Phineas Lyman

General Orders of 1757

Issued by the Earl of Loudoun and Phineas Lyman in the campaign against the

French

Phineas Lyman

General Orders of 1757

Issued by the Earl of Loudoun and Phineas Lyman in the campaign against the French

ISBN/EAN: 9783337425012

Printed in Europe, USA, Canada, Australia, Japan

Cover: Foto ©Suzi / pixelio.de

More available books at **www.hansebooks.com**

GENERAL ORDERS

OF

1757

ISSUED BY

THE EARL OF LOUDOUN

AND

PHINEAS LYMAN

IN THE

CAMPAIGN AGAINST
THE FRENCH

NEW YORK
MDCCCXCIX

Of this book 250 copies only were printed from type January 31, 1899, by The Gilliss Press.

PREFATORY NOTE

THE following General Orders are a full transcript of a Ms. orderly book which recently came into my possession. The manuscript belonged to the regiment of General Phineas Lyman, of Connecticut, one of the commanding officers in the campaign against the French, and a man whose merits and sterling qualities were not recognized by his English colleagues and superiors. The credit that was owing to him was given to others; but a study of the campaign of 1756 shows how ably he performed his part, and how much its success depended upon his efforts.

We cannot seek in orderly books for deeds of bravery, or incidents of battle; but we do find what is of equal interest—the discipline of the camp and the punishment of wrong doing. The dry and somewhat colorless record of the troops from day to day becomes of value when the history of a company or of an army is to be written. Where discipline is maintained and a proper care for the health and morals of the men is bestowed, surely praise is due. In this light the orders hold a high rank as authoritative records, and for this reason I have deemed them worthy of publication.

The editing of this issue was performed by Mr. Worthington C. Ford.

Wm. Seward Webb.

New York, November, 1898.

GENERAL ORDERS
OF
1757

GENERAL ORDERS
OF 1757

By Phinehas Lyman Esqr., Maj^r. Gen^{ll}. and Colonel of the Troops Raised by ye Colony of Connecticut To act in Conjunction with His Majesty's Ragular Troops, Under the command of His Excelency ye Earl of Loudoun, ye Next Campaign.

Order'd

That the Two Companys Quartered By ye River Mount a Guard to consist of one Subaltern Two Sergeants 2 Corporals 1 Drum^r. & Forty Private men To Keep out ten Sentinels To be Relieved Every Two Hours.

That the Two Companys Quartered at or near Hogaboom's Do ye Same.

That Capt Putnam's Company Mount a Guard To Consist of one Searj^t· one Corp^l· & Twenty Men To Keep out Five Senterys to Be Relieved as Above.

All ye guards to Be Relieved at ye Beat of the Troop at 9 o'Clock in ye Morning.

That ye Drums all Beat ye Reveille at Half After Four oclock in ye Morning & Every Company Turn out immediately & Parade on ye Places of Rendezvous where ye officers are to Meet and Call them over & See that ye Men are all clean & well Dress'd & to Note Every Defect, & that Every man Dress Neat & Clean when on Duty.

That ye Commanding officers of Each company See that their Men are Exercised from ten to twelve oClock A.M. and from Four to Six P: M:, that the Places of Parad are Kept clean and Neat.

That the Drums Beat ye Tattoo at Seven oClock at Night & Every Company to turn out on ye Paraid. The officers to Meet em̃ and call em̃ over & as soon as Dismised Every man to Return to His

Quarters & Not to Be Absent without Leave & to Keep still & Behave Orderly.

That No officer or Souldier Goes out of Town without leave from ye Commanding officer.

That ye officers Take care to Be Punctual to the Exact time of Performing Every order, & to see That ye Souldiers Do ye Same, & By No Means To Get into a Loose way of Doing Duty.

That a Return Be Made this Day of Each Company Arrived at Claverack.

That for Every Breach of order ye Offender Be Confined & a Report thereof to Be Made By ye officer of ye Guard as Soon as Relieved.

Given Under My Hand at Fondie's in Claverack ye 2nd Day of May 1757

     P. Lyman

Fondies in Claverack May 3rd 1757

A Regimental Court Martial to set Tomorrow morning at Hogabooms at 8 oClock Consisting of ye following Officers (viz) Capt: Whittelcy President

GENERAL ORDERS OF 1757

Lieut John Durke⎫ Mem- ⎧Lieut Simons
Ens^n. Porter ⎭ bers ⎩Ens^n. Minor
To Try Such Prisoners as Shall be Brought before them.   P Lyman.

Vanantwerp in Scortercook May 16th, 1757.

Parole *London*—Countersign *Courage & Conduct.*

That there Be a Guard Kept here To Consist of one Capt. Two Sub^s, 4 Serg^{ts}, 44 Corp^{ls}, 1 Drum. & 100 Private Men To Be Detached in Proportion out of ye Several Companys Stationd Here, and to Be Posted in ye Following Manner. Viz: The Main Guard To Consist of one Capt: Two Sub^s. 1 Serg^t. 2 Corp^{ls}. 1 Drum & 60 Men—To Be Posted in Som Convenient Place Near ye Mill. A Sergt. Corp^l. & 14 Men To Be Posted at ye House NorthEast From Capt: Fitch's Quarters to Keep out 3 Sentnels at a Time.— A Sergt. Corp^l. & 13 Men to Be Posted at The Top of ye Hill N. East of the orchard To Keep out 3 Sentinels at a Time.— A Sergt. Corpl. & 13 Men To Be Posted Upon ye Hill S.W. of the Mill Pond to Keep out 3 Sentrys at a Time. And the Main Guard To Keep out 15 Sentinels at a Time.

That No Person Go out Hunting Nor over ye River without Leave from ye Commanding off^{r.}

That ye Commanding Off^{r.} of Each Company See that their Mens Cartridges are Examined Every Monday Morning & Return ye Name of those that Have Not their Complement, who are To Be Delt with as Embezzlers of ye Kings Stores Beside three pence Sterling for Each Charge Expended. That ye Off^{r.} See that There Men Don't Do any Damage To Houses Barns Boards or Fences. And any Person that is Found Guilty of the Same Shall Be immediately Confined

That the Names of the Commission off^{ers} & their Rank Be Return.d this Afternoon to ye Adjutant. The Company to Be Exercised as at Claverick.

No Person to Fire off His Piece on any

Account Except that of His Duty against His Enemy.

The Tatoo & Ravilee to Beat as Mention.d in Standing Orders at Claverick & Roll Call &c. P. Lyman

Vanantwerp's in Scortercook May 17th 1757

Parole *Winslow.* Countersign *Courage & Conduct*

That y^e Guards Be Lessoned to the Number of One Sub^n 4 Serj$^{ts.}$ 5 Corp^{ls,} 1 Drum & 60 Men. The Main Guard to Consist of One Sub$^{n.}$ 1 Serj$^{t.}$ 2 Corp$^{ls.}$ 1 Drum & 30 privats. Three Serj$^{t.}$ Guards To Consist of a Serj$^{t.}$ Corp^l & 10 Men Each & that there Be three Relievs of the Sentry that y^e Capt Be Appointed to Go y^e Grand Rounds at 3 oClock in y^e Morning to See that the Sentals are Elert & Watchful on their Posts.

The Serj^{ts} of y^e Several Guards to Make their Reports to y^e Capt. of y^e Main Guard who is to Make His Report to ye off^r of ye Day Mentioning all Casualties that May Happen During His Guard with ye Name of His Prisoners their Crimes By whom Confind & to whom they Belong As soon as Reliev.d And ye off^r of ye Day to the Commanding off^r — the off^r. of the Guard To Go ye Rounds at 12 oClock at Night & a Patrol Betweend Every Relief.—And if any Sentry is Found Asleep or Unfaithful He is to Be Immediately Reliev'd & Confined.   P Lymon

Vanantwerps in Scortercook May 18th 1757

Parole *Winthworth*. That Capt. Putnam and Capt. Jeffery's Company's Mount a Guard To Consist of One Subn. 1 Serj^t. 1 Corp^l. 1 Drum and 30 Men. That Capt. Slapp & Capt. Wells's Company's to Mount a Serj^ts Guard and to Make a Report as Soon as Relieved to ye Sub. who Commands the Guard Mentioning all Causeltys that Shall Happen During His Guard & ye Sub^n to the Capt: Who is Appointed off^r of ye Day & He to Captn

Putnam who is Appointed Commanding Off^r at Vanderhadens.—And that there Be three Relievs of ye Sentries. The Off^r Who Commands ye Guard is to Go ye Rounds at 12 oClock at Night & ye off^r of ye Day at 3 in ye Morning & a Serj^t. or Corp^l. with a File of Men once Betweend Every Relief.

That ye Orderly Serj^ts See that their Men who Mount Guard are well Aquipt Shavd & Decently Dressed Before They March to ye Parade.

The Commanding off^rs of ye Nine Companys Belonging To ye Connecticutt Troops are Desired to Give in a Muster Roll of their Companys as Soon as Possible with the Time of Enlistment & Places of Abode Sick &c. And That an Exact Return Be Made Every Monday Morning to See whether they Have their Number of Cartridges & those that are Deficient May Expect to be delt with as Embezzlers of ye Kings Stores Beside Paying three Pence Sterling for each Charge Expended.

That ye Tents at Venderhadins Be Put out and Dried

As Some Persons Have Hitherto Contrary to Orders Indulgd them Selves in Not Turning out at Roll Calls—For ye Future they who Don't Appear at the Place Appointed as Soon as ye Drum Has Done Beeting Are to Be Confind & tried By a Coort Martial.

A Regimental Coort Martial to Be Held this Afternoon to Consist of ye Following Off^rs Viz:

Capt: Aaron Whittelcy President
Lieut. Durke ⎫ Mem- ⎧ Lieut. Stoton
Lieut. Waterman ⎭ bers ⎩ Ens.^n Minor
To Try Such Prisoners as Shall Be Brought Before them   P Lyman

Vanantwerps in Scortercook May ye 19th 1757

That ye Commanding off^r of Each Company in the Connecticutt Reg^t Se that ye Articles of War Against Mutiny & Desertion are Read at ye Head of their Companys at Least once in Two Months.

GENERAL ORDERS OF 1757

The Orderly Serj.t or Corp.l of Each Company are to Attend at y.e Revallee Every Morning at Relieving the Guards & there to Remain till Dismissd By y.e Adjutant that if any Orders are to Be Deliverd they May Be Ready to Receive them

P. Lymon

Vanantwerps in Scortercok May 20th 1757

Parole *Belcher*

Capt. Fitch off.r of y.e Day Tomorrow. That Guards Be Mounted as Usual & Former Orders Obay.d

Evening Orders. That the Five Companys Now Stationed Here Hold them Selves in Readiness to March Next Day after Tomorrow For Fort-Edward & that they Cook Two Days Provision Befor they March. That My Company Go over ye River this afternoon & Continue there Opposet to Head Quarters & that y.e Men Take Spaciel Care that they leave None of their Provision Behind them

P Lymon

GENERAL ORDERS OF 1757

Vanantwerps in Scortercook   May 21st 1757

Parole *Pownell*.

That y^e Several Companys Belonging to My Reg$^{t.}$ See that they Clean up there Arms This Afternoon & Be Ready to March over ye River if Orderd.

P Lymon

Head Quarters at Saratoge May 23rd 1757

Evening Orders. That the Following Companys Hold them Selves in Readiness to March Early tomorrow Morning for Fort Edward Viz: Gen$^{ll.}$ Lymons Col. Pasons, Capt Putnam's, Capt. Fitch's & Capt Whittlecy's Companys. & 4 Companys to Tarry at Saratoge Till Further Orders or Where M: Lesley Shall Appoint.

That an Offr with 30 Men be detach.d out of y^e 4 Companys to Tarry Here. To March Early Tomorrow Morning with Mr. Lesley.   P Lymon

GENERAL ORDERS OF 1757

Head Quarters Camp at Saratoge May 24th 1757

Parole *Hallyfax*

Capt. Slapp off^r of ye Day

That Lieut Jedediah Waterman with all ye Indians In Capt: Gallup's Company Hold them Selves in Readiness To join the Five Company Orders to Fort Edward

That No Man Go without ye Out Sentrys without His Arms & Liberty from ye Commanding offr. P Lymon

Head Quarters Camp at Saratoge May 25th 1757

Parole *Pitt*

That y^e off^r of y^e Guard See that His Men are Calld Over Morning & Evening & to Exercise them at the Same Time that the Several Companys in Camp are Exercised.

A Regimental Court Martial to Be Held at 11 oClock This Morning in y^e Reg$^{t.}$ Commanded By the Honourable Phineas Lymon Esqr. To Consist of y^e Following Members

GENERAL ORDERS OF 1757

Capt. John Slapp President

Members	
Lieut Samuel Wells	Lieut John Stoton
Lieut Nichola Nichols	Ens.n Elijah Porter

To Try Such Prisoners as Shall Be Brought Before them

       P Lymon

Fort Edward May 28th 1757

Parole *Parker*. Countersn *George*

That ye Commanding offr. of Each Company are to See their Men Have all Good Flints, & if any is Wanting To Give in a Return That they May Be immediately Supplied   P Lymon

Fort Edward May 29th 1757

Parole *Webb* Countersn *Daniel*

That ye Remainder of ye three Companys of the 35 Regt. That Have not as Yet Fired, to Be Ready at 3 oClock This afternoon to Fire at a Mark & Such Men that are on Duty are to Be Reld. till Firing is Over

Twenty Ax Men of the Connecticutt Troops To Go over to the Island Early Tomorrow Morning & 4 Spade Men in Order to Make a Fence Round ye Garden Belonging to the Troops. Two Carpenters will Attend & Shall Shew Them the Manner it is to Be Done.—This Party is to Continue till ye Work is Done

Fort Edward May 30th 1757
    Parole *Hay*
    Countersⁿ *Charles*

Whereas Several Solders of the Garrison Have Been Lately Supplied with Rumm without Pases from their Offr^s Contrary to Orders. It is therefor Repeated that if Any Person Belonging to ye Garrison or Island Shall Presume To Sell any Rumm to ye Troops or to Any of Sr Wm Johnson's Indians Pasing or Repasing they shall Be Tried For Disobedience of orders & Turned out of ye Garrison.

A Capt: Two Sub^s & 70 Men of the Connecticutt Troops To Hold them Selves in Readiness to March this Evening.

That all y*e* Serj*ts* & Corp*ls* in y*e* Connecticutt Reg*t.* y*t.* are of from Duty, Turn out at 6 oClock in y*e* Morning To Be Exercis'd By M*r.* Welch of ye 35*th* Reg*t.* till 7 oClock

That y*e* Commanding off*r* of Each Company Se y*t.* Their Men are Exercised from 4 to 6 oClock in y*e* Afternoon

Fort Edward May 31*st* 1757
    Parole *Cherlston*

That a Detachment of 100 Men Hold them Selves in Readiness To March Tomorrow Morning to y*e* Lake by Break of Day.—Capt. Putnam & Capt. Burgaa's Rangers 30 Men Each The Connecticutt Troops one Capt. One Subn & 40 Men.—

That there Be a Piqt. Guard Raised consisting of one Capt. Two Sub*s.* 2 Serj*ts.* 2 Corp*ls.* 1 Drum*r* & 50 Men to Mount At 7 oClock in y*e* afternoon who are to Lie on their Arms All Night & in Case of any Alarm to Be Ready to Turn out at a Minutes Warning they are likewize to Turn out at Beating y*e* Gen*ll.* in yᵉ Morning & to Peraid At yᵉ Common Plais of Peraid In Order to Escort Waggons &c. And if there Be Any left that are Not Employ'd in That Servis, Upon Hearing yᵉ Genˡˡ in Camp they Are to Repair to yᵉ Plais Appointed for that Porpos.

A Regimental Cort Maretial to Be Held at 11 oClock This Morning to Consist of yᵉ following offʳˢ· Viz.

Captain John Jeffery President

Members:
- Lieut John Durke
- Lieut Robert Durke
- Lieut John Stoton
- Ensⁿˢ Benjamin Howard

To Try Such Prisoners as Shall Be Brought Before them

Fort Edward June 1ˢᵗ 1757

Parole *Greinwich*

A Return of yᵉ Two Ranging Companys to Be Given In immediately to yᵉ Commanding offʳ Making Mention of yᵉ Condition of their Arms Powder Horns Shot Bags and Tomahawks.—

That No Indians Be Suffered to Come onto y^e Island without a written Pass from Gen$^{ll.}$ Webb or S$^{r.}$ W$^m.$ Johnson The off$^{r.}$ of y^e Line Guard is to Report all Passengers that come in or Goes out of y^e Lines to y^e Capt. of y^e Day & all Extraordinarys that May Happen on His Guard.—

A Regimental Coort Maretial To Be Held at 11 oClock This Morning in y^e Reg$^{t.}$ Commanded By y^e Honourable Phinehas Lymon Esqr. To Consist of y^e following off^{rs} Viz.

Capt. Ben Adam Gallup President
Lieut Durke ⎱ Mem- ⎰ Lieut Humphreys
Lieut Simons ⎰ bers ⎱ Ensn Minor
To Try Such Prisoners as shall Be Brought Before them.

Fort Edward June 2nd 1757
Parole *Kensington*. Count^n *Edward*
A Serg$^{t.}$ & twelve Men of ye Connecticutt Troops To Take Post at Fort Ann & to Carry 4 Days Provision with them The Party is to March This Evening &

to Be Relieved Every Fifth Day Till Further Orders.

The Sergt. Commanding y^e Covering Party with the Carpenters is Not to Allow any Fire to Be Lighted Near The Timber that is Prepairing for ye Kings work. And if any is Remaining He is to Use His Utmost Endeavour to Extingish it.

Fort Edward June 3rd 1757
    Parole *Milton.*   Countⁿ *Andrew*

Fort Edward June 4th 1757
    Parole *Athlone*   Countⁿ *George*
Six Men of ye Connecticutt Troops to Hold them Selves In Readiness to March at Beating ye Retreet this Evening To Take 4 Days Provision with them & if they [need] Any Ammunition, A Serg^{t.} of Artillery is Ordered to Provide It on their Giving a Receit for ye Same.—

The off^{rs} of all Guards to Give strict Orders to Confine all Solders that shall Be Seen Wadeing or Swimming in the River in their Regimental Cloths, or Fishing from Under ye cover of the Musketary of ye Garrison.

Fort Edward June 5th 1757

    Parole *Ergile*   Countⁿ *Archable*

    A Subⁿ 1 Sergt. 1 Corp^l & 30 Men of ye Connecticutt Troops to Hold them Selves in Readiness to March at an Hours Warning. they will be joined by a Party of Capt. Putnams Rangers & are to be under His Com^{d.} Who will Give Directions How Much Provision they shall Carry with them.

    R. O. That ye Commanding off^r of Each Company In ye Connecticutt Reg^{t.} Return an Exact Muster Roll of their Companys to ye Commanding off^r Specifying Fit for Duty Sick on Com^{d.} Dead Deserted Never joined &c. in Diferent Colems By them Selves.—In Order to Prepare for a Muster Tomorro in ye afternoon By ye Gen^{ll.} Order

        Timy Hierlihy Adjutant

Fort Edward June 6th 1757

 Parole *Abercrombie*

 A Capt. Two Sub^s & 60 Men of ye Connecticutt Troops To Hold them Selves in Readiness to March at an Hours Warning to Escort ye Kings Stores to ye Lake.

 Gen^ll. Lymons Reg^t. to Be Under arms tomorrow at 5 oClock in ye Afternoon in Order to Be Muster'd & to Hear ye Articles of War Read to Them viz. ye 2nd & 6th Sections & 4th & 5 Articles of ye Articles of War The Col: or Commanding off^r of ye Reg^t is to Make Constant Report of their Strength to Maj^r. Gen^ll. Webb.

Fort Edward June 7th 1757

 Parole *Hardy*

 That a Serj^t. & 10 Men of ye Connecticutt Troops Take Post at Fort Ann Tomorrow Morning & Take 5 Days Provision with them.—

 The Men Warn'd to Go for Bark to Peraide Early Tomorrow Morning with

yᵉ Other Partys, and a Detachment from yᵉ Piqt to cover them.
Capt. for yᵉ Day Tomorrow Capt Fossh

Fort Edward June 8ᵗʰ 1757.
Parole *Lisbon* Countn *John*
It is Majʳ Fletcher's Orders that when any Discovery of The Enimy Be Made Either By Track Sight or Firing of Small Arms the Commanding offʳˢ of yᵉ Party that mak Discovery is immediately to Send one Man or More as He Shall Think Proper in Order to Acquaint ye Commanding offʳˢ as Soon as Possible.—
The Covering Party at yᵉ Brickill to Take Post within The Stockaids at yᵉ Retreet Beating & Place yᵉ Sentrys yᵉ Inside & Make as little Noice as Possible During yᵉ Night they will Be Relᵈ· Every Morning By yᵉ New Covering Party who is to Take Post in Like Manner Till Further Orders.—All Sentrys are to Be Vegilent on their Posts Neither are they to Smoke Tobacco or Suffer any Noice to Be Made Near them they are Not to Set

down Nor to Lay their Arms Out of their Hands Not to Sleep But to Keep Moving aBout their Posts—if the Weather will Allow of it they are to Keep a Watchful Eye over ye Things Commited to their Charge & Not to Suffer any of them To Be Moved or Taken away till they Have orders from ye Corp^l.

Fort Edward June 12th 1757
    Parole *Johnson*
    A Capt. Two Sub^s & 60 Men of ye Connecticutt Troops To March Tomorrow Morning to ye Lake as an Escort to ye Kings Teems.

    The Piq^t within ye Lines are for ye Future to Ground their Arms upon Forked Sticks, & a Sentry to Be Plaisd Over them. Where they are to Remain with ye Off^rs Fuzie in ye Front. Except it Be in Rainy Weather That they May Upon ye Least alarm Be Ready to March emediately.

    When any Discovery is Made with Respect to the Enemy By Night By yᵉ Redout Guard or Advaincd Sentrys, Notice is to Be Emmediately Given to the Sentry at yᵉ Flag Staff Who is to Call to yᵉ Corpl. of The Fort Guard in Order that yᵉ Capt. of Sᵈ· Guard May Be Acquainted with it Who is Forthwith to Make [report] To yᵉ Commanding Offʳ·

Fort Edward June 13ᵗʰ 1757.
    Parole *Standwix*.
    The Commanding offʳ of Companys are to Take Perticular Cair that their Men are Kept Compleat And all Serjᵗˢ & Corpˡˢ to Inspect into their Ammunition in Order to Se that they Have 24 Rounds of Powder & Ball & a Good Flint in His Pies.—
    All offʳˢ Mounting Guard Detachments out Partys &c. are Before they March from yᵉ Peraid to Examen their Mens Ammunition Agreeable to yᵉ Above Orders—& if any Deficiency is Found The Adjᵗ is Emmediately to Be Acquainted with it in Order that yᵉ Serjᵗ or Corpl Who Peraded yᵉ Men May Be Found out

Fort Edward June 14th 1757
    Parole *Lyman* Countn *George*

Fort Edward June 18th 1757
    Parole *New York* Count *Charles*

Fort Edward June 19th 1757
    Parole *Home* Countn *Robert*

It is Majr Fletcher's orders that when any Firing is Herrd By ye Patroling Partys Detach.d from ye Piqt. or Advains.d Guards, the Former is Emmediately to March & Make Discovery.

Fort Edward June 20th 1757
    Parole *Goff* Countn *Edward*

Agreeable to ye Genll Orders the Following is a Ragulation for Provisions as Settled By ye Contractors with His Excelency ye Earl of Louden.

The Allowance for one Person for Seven Days Going on aScout In Lieu of ye three Pintes of Pees 6 oz. of Butter for ye ½ lb of Rice they are to Have 1 lb 3 oz. of Pork, which Makes their Weeks allowance to Be 7 lb of Bread 5 lb. 3 oz. of Pork.

Two Serjts 2 Corp[ls] & 24 Men to Be Ready to March this Evening at Sunset they are to Carry 7 days Allowance with them Agreable to y[e] Above Orders— & When they are Ready They are to Wait on y[e] Commanding off[r] for Orders.

It is Maj[r.] Fletchers Orders that y[e] Commanding off[r] of the Diferent Corps Se that y[e] Streets of their Respective Encampments Be Swept Clean Every Day & that an off[r] Of a Company Visit y[e] Mens Tents in Order to Se that they Are Kept as Clean as Possable & if any of y[e] Tents are Found after this Day with any Filth or Durt in them the Visiting off[r] is Emmediately to Order S[d] Tent to be Struct & Cleaned—& the Men Who He Judges to Be Guilty of this Neglect are Emmediately to Be Confined for Disobedience of Orders.

The N Hampshire Troops Under

Com^d of Col. Goff to Peraid as Soon as Possable Betweend ye Two Encampments Without ye Lines in Order to Be Musterd & Hear the Articles of War Read to them.—

R. O. That ye Commanding off^r of Each Company in the Connecticutt Reg^t· Make a Return by 12 oClock tomorrow of ye Servis Size age & Country of ye Commissn.d Non Commission.d & Private Men Belonging to their Respective Companys.—

Countrys Viz. England, Scotland, Ireland, Amaircae, Foreigners, Natives of Amaircae &c.—

Their Age from 18 years & Under to 55 & Upward—

Their Size from 5 Feet 6 Inches & Under to 6 Feet 2 Inches & upward—

The Time of their Servis in Each Reg^t· from one Year & Under to Thirty Five Years & Upward.—

Capt. Fitch offr of ye Day Tomorrow Who is to Visit ye Tents—Lieut. Castle ye Line Guard.

Fort Edward June 21st 1757.

Parole *Montgomery* Cn. Dance.

The Commanding off rs of ye Different Corps are to Send their Returns agreeable to ye Form Deliverd to ye Brig-aid-Majr. as Soon as Possable in order that they May Be Forwarded To Capt. Cuningham one of Lord Louden's Aid-De-Camps.—

Whereas Several Solders Have Been Observed to Strool from Under The Cover of ye Musketary of ye Camps & Garrison Contrary to Orders—It is therefore Maj:r Fletchers Orders that No Solder for ye Future Presume to Strool from Under ye Cover of ye Muskatary as Afor.Sd. without Perticular Liberty as The Col: or Commanding offr. of ye Regt. or Detachments Who are to Be Answerable to ye Commanding offr. for all Such as they Shall Think Proper to Give Lieve too.—

R. O. That ye Commanding offr. of Each of ye Connecticutt Companys Se that one of their Subn. offrs. By Turns Se their Company Exercised at 4 oClock Every Afternoon.

As it Heatherto Has Been Neglected to Make a Return Every Monday Morning of ye Names of those that Wont Cartrages & what Number—It is Gen^{ll} Lyman's Orders that ye Clerke of Each Company Do it with out Fail and any that Disobey this order shall Suffer Accordingly.—

Capt. Slapp off^r· of ye Day Tomorrow—

Lieut Wells ye Line Guard—

Fort Edward June 22nd 1757
Parole *Webb*—Daniel

Whereas His Majesties Inginear Hath Made Complaint to The Commanding off^r· that ye Tools Deliver.d out to ye Troops are Not Brought in When ye Work is Done—It is therefor Maj.^{r} Fletchers Orders that all Tools of Whatever Kind that Has already or May Be Delivered out on Account of His Majesties Service Shall for ye Future be return.d After S^d· Work is

Finish.d & if any of S.d Tools are Left or Damag.d they are to Be Made Good By those that Break or Loos them.

As Maj.r Gen.ll Webb is Daily Expected at Fort Edward Maj.r Fletcher Recommends it to the Diferent Commanding off.rs of Reg.ts & Ranging Companys to Se that their Respective Incampments Are Kept Clean as Posable Agreable to Former Orders.—At ye Beet of Two long Ruffels all guards are to turn out with Rested arms, on ye Gen.ll Approaching & in Cais He Chuses to Go Along y.e Lines of y.e Different Encampments—the Commanding offr. of S.d Corps or Detachments is Emmediately to order a Long Ruff to Be Beet Upon Which y.e Men are Emmediately to Turn out with their Side Arms— the Piq.t to Draw out in y.e Senter of y.e Reg.t Advainsing Before y.e Lines with their Proper off.rs, & y.e off.rs are to Advains Before y.e Piq.t in Two Ranks according to Seniority.—

R. O. That a Sub.n of Each Company in y.e Connecticutt Reg.t Se that their

Mens arms are Kept Clean within & without & Vieu them at Roll Calling Every Night & any that Neglect to Do it is Emmediately to Be Confin.d for Disobedience Of Orders.

Capt. Jeffery off.r of y.e Day tomorrow. Lieut. John Durke y.e Line Guard

Fort Edward June 23.rd 1757.
Parole *Brunswick.* Coun.n *Thomas.*
The Sentry at y.e Gate & y.e In Side are Not for y.e Future To Suffer any Person to Pass or Repass till y.e Draw Bridge is Finish.d.

R. O. The Commanding off.r of Each Company to take Cair That their Men Appear as Clean & Deasent as Possable

Capt. Wells off.r of y.e Day Tomorrow —L.t Fitch y.e Line Guard

Fort Edward June 26.th 1757.
Parole *Middlesex.* Coun.t *Ralph.*
R. O. Capt. Slapp off.r of y.e Day tomorrow
Lieut Humphrys y.e Line Guard

Fort Edward June 27th 1757

Parole *Kensington*

That ye Adjutants of ye Different Reg^{ts} are to Attend ye Brigaid-Maj:^r for Orders Every Day at 11 oClock at ye Off^{rs} Garden.—

Every Reg^{t.} to Send in a Return as Soon as Possable of The Present Strength of their Field off^{rs} Cap^{s.} Lieut^{s,} Ens^{ns,} Serj^{ts,} Corp^{ls} Drum^{rs,} & Effective Private Men & Such Reg^{ts} as Have Any on out Commands Are to Specify Where they are Gon, & when they Expect to return.—A Return is Likewize to Be Given in of ye Number of Artificers in Each Reg^{t.} In which Return is to Be Specified ye Number and Perticular Traids of those Who are Constantly Employ.d in ye Kings Work. —Also a Return to Be Given in of ye Names of all ye off^{rs} in Each Reg^{t.} With ye Dates of their Several Commissions, all ye Above Returns are to Be Sign'd By ye Commanding off^{r.} of Each Reg^{t.} — & ye Gen^{ll} Desires that they May Be Vary Exact & as Soon as they are Made

Out they are to Be Sent to ye Brigaid Maj.^{r}.

R. O. That ye Commanding off^{rs} of Each Company In ye Connecticutt Reg^t. Se that ye Above returns Are Sent in to ye Adj^t. as Soon as Possable.

Tis Gen^{ll}. Lyman's Orders that Jonathan Tuttle of Capt. Putnam's Company is Appointed Corp^l. and is to Be Obayd as Such.

Fort Edward June 28th 1757
Parole *Norfolk*

When ye Assisting Debuty Quarter Master Gen^{ll} Has mark.d out ye Lines of ye Incampment ye Several Reg^{ts} are to Pitch their Tents—Accordingly ye Commending Off^r of Each Corp is to be Answerable to ye Gen^{ll} that their Reg^{ts} Incamp Proper, & on ye Ground Assign.d them By M^r. Lesley. & any Tents Pich.d Irragular will Be Order.d to Be Struct. No Hutts will Be Allow.d off. Upon any Account within ye Lines—and the Men's Kitchens are to Be Built in yᵉ Front Without yᵉ Lines—the Commanding offʳˢ of Each Regᵗ· are Likewise to Be Answerable to yᵉ Genˡˡ that yᵉ Streets are Kept Clean as Possable and yᵉ Dust Assign.d By Clearing the Camp is Not to be Buried But Carried & thrown into yᵉ River, for which Porpos Genˡˡ Webb will Order a Proper Number of Wheel Barrows or Basketts.—

yᵉ 35th Regᵗ to Muster Tomorrow Morning Emmediately After yᵉ Guards are Reliev.d—

The 62nd Regᵗ· & Independant Companys to Take yᵉ Guard in yᵉ Fort & yᵉ Redoubt Upon yᵉ Artillery Tomorrow Which Duty is to be Repaid them By yᵉ 35th Regᵗ·

Fort Edward June 29th 1757
 Parole *Northamptonshire*

Whatever offʳ or other Gentleman in yᵉ Camp Have any Letters to Go to Albany on Demands they are Desired to Send them to Capt. Bartman at yᵉ Genˡˡˢ Quarters at Fort Edward every Tuesday

& Friday Mornings at 10 oClock Exactly—

Fort Edward June 30th 1757
    Parole *Northumberland*
The Carpenters and ye Men ordered to Make Fashiens with the Partys to Cover them are to Take their Breakfast with them as they are Not to Return to ye Camp till Dinner—

Fort Edward July 1st 1757
    Parole *Notinghamshire*
The Necessary Houses Belonging to ye Several Regtts o Be Emmediately fil.d Up & New Ones Dug Six feet Deep & about 100 yards in ye Front of ye Respective Encampments. Each Regt Every Evening to Cover ye Bottom of them over with Fresh Earth—& New ones to Be Dug Every Wheek & ye Old ones to Be fil.d Up—The Commanding offr of Each Regt. to Be Answerable to ye Genll that this order is Strictly Obay.d
    That ye Commanding offr of Each

Reg^t Now Encampt at Fort Edward are Emmediately to Appoint a Setler or a Person to Supply ye Reg^t with Necessary Stors The Name of which Person So Appointed is to Be Given In to Mr. Lesley Assisting Debuty Quarter Master General And all other Persons Who are Setlers or Followers of ye Several Reg^{ts} are Under their Protection their Names are Likewise to Be Returned to Mr. Lesley. ye Cors which They are to Follow when any Setler has Occation for a Supply of Stors from Albany or Elce Where for y^e Use of Which Reg^t He Belongs— He is to Give an Account of ye Different Speties He Wonts Especially Speritous Liquers, to ye Commanding off^r of y^e Reg^t for His Approbation & when that is obtaine.d y^e Quarter Master of y^e Regt is to Apply to M$^r.$ Lesley Who will Grant them a Pass to go to Albany By y^e Different Posts Who are to Shew y^e Pass to Capt: Cristie Who will Grant Him another For His Return.—

No Setlar Shall Presume to Pitch His

tent or to Break any Ground or Build a Hutt, Either Within or without the Lines without First Applying to Mr. Lesley, Under Penalty of Having all their Liquers Stove & their stors Demolish'd - - - - All Setlers Followers Waggoners of ye Army or Others are Upon their Arrival to ye Camp to Apply to Mr Lesley & Acquaint Him of their Business Where they are Going & How long they will Tarry Here And they are Not to Leave ye Camp Upon any Pretence With out His Pass Either up or Down ye Country & all Persons Coming into ye Camp with Stors & Have Got Passes from M^r· Christie are also to apply to M^r· Lesley Who will Acquaint them of ye Commanding off^{rs} Orders Conserning them—

Fort Edward July 2nd 1757.
    Parole *Oxfordshire*
    A Piq^t· to Mount Every Night Consisting of Two Capt^s Six Sub^s· 8 Serj^{ts} 8 Corp^{ls} & 192 Men to Peraid at ye Grand

Peraid at yᵉ Firing of yᵉ Evening Gun.—
Mr. Lesley A. D. Q. M. G. will Mark
out a Proper Plais Upon yᵉ Right & Left
of yᵉ Camp where yᵉ Piqᵗ is to Divide &
Lay out - - - -Each Corp to Send a Number of Tents in Proportion to the Number
of Men they Give Allowing 5 Men to
Each Tent.—The Capt of Each Piqᵗ is to
Be Answerable to yᵉ Genˡˡ that His Piqᵗ· is
Constantly Kept togather Ready to Turn
out on yᵉ Shortest Notis.—The Men for
ye Piqᵗ· are Always to Bring with them
To yᵉ Peraid their Provision Cook.d for
yᵉ Next Day as the Capts are Not to allow
Any Man to Stur from His Command on
any Pretence Whatever.—

After Orders. The Commanding offʳ
of yᵉ Different Regᵗˢ to Be Answerable to
yᵉ Genˡˡ that yᵉ Men Belonging to their
Respective Corps When Order.d for Duty
Peraid in Good order & Each Man be
Provided with 24 Rounds of Powder &
Ball—& Such Men as Have No Cartrage
Boxes, are to Have their Cartrages Done
Up in Small Parsels & Produce them to

ye Off^r of ye Piq^t. When He Examens them.—And it is Recommended To y Commanding off^rs of ye Different Reg^ts to Take Perticular Cair that their Men Don't Waist their Ammunition, for an account is Taken By ye Artilery of ye Quantity Deliver.d to Each Corps. Whatever Ammunition is Not Expended in ye Servis will Be Charged to Each Reg^t & they will Be Obliged to Pay for their Deficiencys Occasion.d By Waist or Neglect.—

The Capts of ye Two Piq^ts are to Make Seperate Reports to ye Gen^ll when Reliev.d & Each Capt: is to Acquaint Him Whether He Has Had Occation To Expend any Ammunition & What Quantity.—

The Quarter Masters of ye Several Reg^ts to Attend Mr. Lesley an Hour Before Sun Set this Afternoon—

Fort Edward July 3rd 1757.
  Parole *Northumberland*

Fort Edward July 4th 1757.
  Parole *Amsterdam*

Fort Edward July 5th 1757

    Parole *Summersetshire*

    A Man of Each Mess of ye 35th Regt. & of ye Detachment of ye 62nd Reg^t Who are in Garrison at Fort-Edward To attend ye Gardner at 10 oClock Tomorow Morning Who will Deliver them out Vegatables to serve The Reg^{ts}.—

    The Commanding off^{rs} of ye Different Reg^{ts} to Send to M^r· Furnis Contractor of ye Ordnance to Know what Time He will Appoint to Receive their Damaged Cartrages & Spair Bullets, for which He will Give a Recait.—

    The Men Belonging to ye Provensial Reg^{ts} who are Appointed to Do ye Duty of Rangers are to Be Emmediately Supplyd with Leather Shot Bags & Powder Horns to Carry their Ammunition in

Fort Edward July 6th 1757.

    Parole *Windsor*

    A Return to Be Given in as Soon as Possable to ye Maj^r Brig.-Aid Sign'd By ye Commanding off^{rs} of Each Reg^t of yᵉ Names of yᵉ Ships Carpenters & Salers or Men Used to Boating, that are in Each Corps, & if any of yᵉ above Men are Employ.d By ye Inginear, they are be Included in yᵉ Return, and The Number to Be Specified at yᵉ Bottom—

Mʳ· Roger Morris Majʳ· of Brig-Aid

Fort Edward July 7ᵗʰ 1757.

Parole *Stafford-shire*

Lieut. Vaniggan of yᵉ 62nd Regᵗ is Appointed To Do yᵉ Duty of an Artillery offʳ & is Not to Do Duty in this Corp But to Encamp with yᵉ Train & Be Under yᵉ Com.ᵈ of Capt. Ord.

When Ever any Regᵗ· Wants Ammunition a Demand is to Be Made in Writeing Sign'd By the Commanding offʳ of yᵉ Regᵗ of yᵉ Number of Cartrages Powder & Ball that is Wanted.—When & What Number of Cartrages they Lost, and How They Have Ben Expended.— All Returns Whatever To be Sign.d By yᵉ Commanding offʳ of Each Regᵗ·

The Provensial Regᵗˢ to Make a Return as Soon Possable of ye Number of Arms out of Repair Specifying ye Different Deficiencies of Each Firelock.

Fort Edward July 8th 1757.
   Parole *Suffolk*
   A Return of ye Number of Inlisted Women & their names Belonging to ye Different Reg^{ts} to Be Given in as Soon as Possable to Capt. Bartmon (Aid-De-Camp to Gen^{ll} Webb.) This Return to Be Signed By ye Commanding off^r of Each Corp.

Fort Edward July ye 9th 1757.
   The Provensial Reg^{ts} to Deliver their Firelocks y^t Want Mending on Monday Morning Next at 7 oClock To Capt. Ord (Commanding off^r of ye Artilery) who will Give Directions for there Being Emmediately Repair.d.—
   A Gen^{ll} Cort Mareschal of ye Line Consisting of one Field off^r 8 Capt^s of ye Ragulars & Four Capt^s of the Provensials To Set on Monday Morning Next at

8 oClock To Try all Such Prisoners as Shall Be Brought Before them.—

 Lieut. Col: Young President—

 Capt. Woodall Judge Advocate—

An off.^r of Each Company to Examen ye Men's Ammunition Every Evening at Gun Firing & a Return to Be Given in Emmediately After to ye Gen^ll of ye State of their Ammunition Sign.d By the Commanding Off.^r Specifying if any Cartrages Be Wanting How ye Deficient one's Have Ben Expended.—

 The Men for Guard in Camp ye Covering & Working Party's to Lode their First Cartrages with Runing Ball for Which Porpos a Proper Proportion of Powder & Ball will Be Deliv.d to Each Corp from ye Artilery.—

Fort Edward July 10th 1757.

 Parole *Sussex*.

 That ye Men for ye Covering Partys with Arms Be Peraided with Powder & Ball till a Proper Number of Powder Horns & Shot Bags Be Provided.—The

GENERAL ORDERS OF 1757

Piq^t & Working Partys are to Peraid with 24 Rounds.

Fort Edward July 11th 1757.
    Parole *Warwickshire.*
    Every Corp is to Appoint a Proper Person to Attend & Receive ye Letters for their Respective Reg^{ts} that Com By ye Post, Which Person is to Pay for those that are Cleard By ye Post Master at Albony & ye Maj^{r.} Brigaid will Take Cair to Send & acquaint ye Reg^{ts.} when ever ye Post Coms in.

Fort Edward July 12th 1757
    Parole *Westmoreland.*
    When Ever any offr Confins a Solder Whether Belonging to ye Ragular Troops or Provensiels the Solder is to Be Sent to ye Quarter Guard of ye Reg^{t.} He Belongs to with ye Crime in Writeing Signed By ye off^r Who orders Him Confin.d—& No Guard is to Receive a Prisoner with out His Crime in Writeing.—

To Prevent ye Inconveniencies arising of ye Solders Not Knowing of ye off^rs of ye Provensiels — Tis Maj^r. Gen^ll Webbs Orders that No off^r Stur out of ye Incampment of His own Reg^t. without Puting on His Sword.

Fort Edward July 15th 1757.
Parole *Wiltshire*

A Cort Mareschal to Consist of one Capt. & Four Subs. To Set Tomorrow Morning at ye Presidents Tent at 10 oClock To Try a Serjt of ye 62nd Regt. Confined By an off^r of the Massachusetts Reg^t. — The 35th Reg^t gives a Capt.— ye 62 Two Sub^s., ye Massachusetts Reg^t. Two Sub^s.

Tis ye Gen^lls Posative Orders that No off^r Solder or Any other Person Belonging to ye Army presume to Give Or Sel any Liquer to ye Indians Upon any Pretence Whatever.— This Order to Be Read to ye Men this Evening at Gun Firing In Presence of an off^n of a Company.

Fort Edward July 14th 1757.
   Parole *Worcestershire*
   Two Men of Each Corp To Peraid Tomorrow Morning At Such an Hour as Capt. Ord shall Appoint at ye Head of ye Artilery Park, to Be Employ.d in Making Up Cartrages, & they are to Be Continued Till Further Orders.

Fort Edward July 15th 1757.
   Parole *Middlesex*

Fort Edward July 16th 1757.
   Parole *Sterling*.

Fort Edward July 17th 1757.
   Parole *Cardiganshire*
   A Cort Mareschal To Set Tomorrow Morning at ye President's Tent Consisting of one Capt. & 4 Subs To Try a Soldier of ye 60th Regt Confin.d By an offr of ye Massachusetts Regt. —The 35th Regt. Gives a Capt. ye 60th Regt 2 Subs. — ye Massachusetts 2 Subs.

Fort Edward July 18th 1757.

Parole *Carmarthenshire*

When Ever Two or More of yᵉ Independant Companys are Joind Together, they are to Look Upon them Selves as a Corp & Not to act as Seperate Companys & all Returns Reports &c. are to Be Made to & Signed By yᵉ Commanding offʳ of yᵉ Whol.—

Mʳ· Lesley A. D. Q. M. G. will shew yᵉ Troops at Distance from yᵉ Lines & yᵉ Grount where they Are to Dig their Kitchings & Necessary Houses & Every Corp is To Take Cair Not to Interfear With yᵉ Ground Either in yᵉ Front or Rear of yᵉ Camp Upon yᵉ Right or Left.—

The Provensial Regᵗ· are To Give In a Return of their Strength Every 15ᵗʰ & 30ᵗʰ of Each Month According To yᵉ Form Lately Given them By the Majʳ Brigaid.—This To Be a Standing Order and The Genˡˡ Expects yᵗ yᵉ Commanding offʳ of Each Regᵗ will Be Vary Perticular in Sending their Returns to yᵉ Majʳ· Brig-Aid on yᵉ Above Mention.d Days.

R. O. That yᵉ Men Belonging To yᵉ Connecticutt Regᵗ When Worn.d for Duty Appear on ye Peraid with Shoes & Stockens on & their Trowsers Wash.d Clean—& Any Person yᵗ Disobays this Order will be Emmediately Confin.d—

Fort Edward July 19ᵗʰ 1757.

Parole *Cornervanshire*

The Quarter Masters of yᵉ Different Corps are to Inform them Selves from Mʳ· Lesley A. D. Q. M. G. Where yᵉ Ground is Mark.d out for yᵉ New Buriing Yard, & For yᵉ Future yᵉ Troops are Not To Dig Graves Any Where Elce Under Panelty of Being Oblig.d To fill Them Up Again—

A Regimental Cort Mareschal to Be Held in Genˡˡ Lymon's Regᵗ at 2 oClock this Afternoon.

Capt. Hitchcock President
Lieut. Nichols ⎫ Mem ⎧ Lieut. John Durke
Lieut. Wells ⎭ bers ⎩ Lieut. Harding

GENERAL ORDERS OF 1757

To Try Such Prisoners as Shall Be Brought Before them.

Fort Edward July 21st 1757.
   Parole *Flintshire*
   The Forts at Saratoge & Still Water are To Be Reliev.d Tomorroe By a Detachment from yᵉ Whol Lines which is To Peraid Tomorrow Morning By 5 oClock at yᵉ Grand Paraid. The Men have To Take their Tents & Camp Necessarys with them Which will Be Carry.d Down By yᵉ Teams Going Down To Saratoge. Each Man is to Be Provided with 24 Rounds of Powder & Ball.—
   The Ragular Troops are To Send a Fornights Subsistence with there Men of their Respective Regᵗˢ which is To Be Paid In to an offʳ of Each Corp or To a Serjᵗ Where No offʳ is Furnish.d
   The Provencial Regᵗ are for yᵉ Future To Give Their Proportion of offʳˢ & Men To yᵉ Fort Redoubt and Other Camp Guards—it is therefor Recommended to yᵉ Commanding offʳ of yᵉ Provencial

Reg.t To Take Cair y.t y.e Men for those Dutys Appear Clean & in Good Order.—

R. O. Tis Gen.ll Lymon's Orders y.t Serj.t Jos:h Comstock of Capt: Fitch's Company Be Reduc.d To y.e Ranks & Do Duty as Such.

Fort Edward July 22nd 1757.

Parole *Glanmorganshire*

R. O. That ye Men Who are Worn.d for Guard Appear Clean Deasent & Well Shav.d with Ramrods a Proper Length for Their Guns. & that Every Man Be Acquipt with Ammunition—& ye Orderly Corp.l Who March their Men To the Peraid are to Se y.e these Orders are Comply.d with.

That all y.e Men of from Duty Turn out at 4 oClock In y.e Afternoon Every Day to Be Exercis.d Till Six By an off.r Appointed for that Porpos.—

Fort Edward July 23rd 1757.

Parole *Montgomemoryshire*

The Artilery To Send a Field Pies

to y ͤ Fort Emmediately Which is to Be Mounted on y ͤ N. E. Bastien where the Flag Staff is Plais.d & In Cais it Shold be found Necessary To Turn out the Lines, a Cannon will Be Emmediately Fired on y ͤ Bastien & a Flag Histed Upon which Every Reg ͭ ˙ is to Turn out at y ͤ Head of their Incampments & to Divide them Selves Along y ͤ Intrenchment as Far as their Tents Extend.—At y ͤ Same Time the Off ͬˢ To Be Plais.d at y ͤ Head of their Several Companys & there Remain till they Receive Further Orders. & Neither off ͬ Nor Soldier is To Stur from His Post Unles He Receivs y ͤ Gen ˡˡ ˢ Perticular Orders, Except one off ͬ from Each Corp who y ͤ Commanding off ͬ is to Send to Attend y ͤ Gen ˡˡ ˙

In Cais of Any Firing in y ͤ Wood y ͤ Picq ͭ is Emmediately To Advains & Soport y ͤ Party y ͭ is Attacked.

The Rangers are Likewise To Turn out at ye Same Time, with y ͤ Off ͬˢ at y ͤ Head of their Companys And are To March With y ͤ First Advainc.d Picq ͭ And as yᵉ Rangers will Extend them Selves on yᵉ Flanks of yᵉ Picqᵗ, The Partys that May Be Order.d Afterwards out to join them are To Take Perticular Cair Not to Fire Upon them.

The Picqᵗ of yᵉ Next Day to Peraid Every Evening at yᵉ Same Time with yᵉ Mounting Picqᵗ· That they May be In Readiness to March To Sustain yᵉ Other Picqᵗ on to Go on any other Servis That May Be Requir.d.—And Upon An A larm they Are Emmediately To Turn out & to March To the Grand Peraid & there Wait Till Further Orders.—

Upon Firing ye Alaram Gun as Soon as yᵉ Troops Have Taken their Posts yᵉ 35ᵗʰ Regᵗ is to Send a Company yᵉ 60th Regᵗ· three Companys the Independants one Company Into yᵉ Fort And The provencial Troops are Likewise To Furnish For this Service one Capt. Six Subˢ· 8 Serjᵗˢ 8 Corpˡˢ & 150 Private Men. The Perticular Proportion for Each Corp will be Demanded By yᵉ Majᵣ-Brig-Aid, and is to Be Furnish.d Emmediately When

GENERAL ORDERS OF 1757

yͤ Above Detachments join yͤ Company of yͤ Ragulars & March into yͤ Fort— the Whol is to Be Under yͤ Command of yͤ Eldest offʳ· who will Dispose of them Along yͤ Paripats.— The Artilery at yͤ Same Time to Send an offʳ & a Proper Number of Men to Manage yͤ Guns within yͤ Fort.—

The Ambersears in yͤ Lines to Be Emmediately Got Ready & Platforms Prepair.d To Receive yͤ Iron 4 Po:ˢ & Upon yͤ Above Guns Being Fired the Artilery is To Send Two Brass Twelve Pounders to yͤ Ground Barrear & Two To yͤ Head of yͤ Royˡ Americans & one Brass Six Pounder to Each of yͤ Openings of the Lines.—

These Orders To Be Read & Explained to yͤ Men By an offʳ of a Company this Evening at Gun Firing and yͤ Genˡˡ Expects that they will Be Punctually Comply.d with and No Person is to Presume To Make a Fals Alarm or to Order yͤ Lines to Turn out But Upon a Proper Signal Above Mention.d And In

Cais of any Shot Being Fired No off' Nor Soldier is to Stur out of ye Lines Unless He is Part of a Detachment or orderd out Under Penelty (if a Commission.d off') of Being Put Under an Erest, & if an Uncommission.d off' or Soldier of being Sevearly Punish.d- - - And After ye Larem Gun is Fired No Soldier is to offer to Quit His Corp Upon any Pretence Whatsoever Under Pain of Death.—

When Ever ye Lines is order.d To Turn out By ye Signal of Alarm the Men are to Be Drawn Up along ye Intrenchment But Not Suffer.d to Mount ye Bank Till order.d By ye Commanding off' of ye Corp they Belong too.

Fort Edward July 24th 1757.
Parole *Pembrookshire.*
A Return to Be Given in Emmediately of ye Men kild Wounded or Mising, & a Return of the Arms & Accotroments Lost be ye Troops as Likewise a Return of all ye Arms Found Belonging to ye Enimy in ye Attact of ye Covering Party

and Workmen Yesterday—this Return To Be Signed By the Commanding off^r of Each Corp.—

Any Soldier that is Sent to ye Gen^{ll} Hospital—The Commanding off^r of ye Corp To which He belongs are To Send a Sertificet with them in Writeing which Is To Be Deliver.d to ye Clerke of ye Hospital.

No Setler Whatsoever is To Sel any Rhum or other Sort of Sparitus Liquers, To any Soldier Whether Belonging To ye Ragular or Provencial Troops Under Penalty of Being Turn.d out of y^e Camp & Having all Their Liquers Taken from them.—

The Following Detachment To Peraid Tomorrow Morning at Gun Firing at y^e Grand Peraid in Order to March To Fort-Wm. Henry, Viz: the Grannidear Company of y^e 60th Reg^t· y^e Grannidear Company of y^e N. York Reg^t & 1 Capt. 6 Subs. 7 Serj$^{ts.}$ Corp$^{ls.}$ & 143 Privats of y^e Provencials.

R. O. That Each Company in y^e Connecticutt Reg^t Give In a List of Such off^rs & Soldiers who were on y^e Picq^t. Yesterday in y^e Front of y^e Ingagement Under y^e Command of Capt: Litler, And also those that were of y^e Party to Cover y^e Carpenters Yesterday.—This is to Be Don Emmediately & also a Return of ye Number of Arms Mising & Found.

Fort Edward July 25th 1757.
    Parole *Webb*.
    Lieut. Dalyell of ye 60th Reg^t is Appointed to Act as Brig-Aid-Maj^r & is to Be Obay.d as Such.
    The Capt^s. of ye Ranging Companys Incamp.d Without ye Lines, are to Make a Thorough Inspection In to ye Stait of their Mens Arms Ammunition *&c.* & To Se that Every Man is Compleated with 24 Rounds Agreable To Former Orders—& if there are any Men at Presant among ye S^d Companys that are Judg.d By their Cap^ts as Unfit for that Servis they are Forthwith To Be Exchang.d for others

of their Respective Corps who are To Take Perticular Cair To Send Good arms with them.—

Fort Edward July 26th 1757
    Parole *Howe*.

No Soldier on any Pretence Whatsoever to Strool From ye Camp or Be Seen in ye River from Under ye Cover of ye Muskatary of ye Line or Fort.—

The Detachment at ye Half Moon To Be Reliev.d Tomorrow Morning By ye Provencial Troops & they are to Peraid By Gun Firing.—This Detachment is to Consist of One Capt. Four Subs. 5 Serjts 5 Corpls & 115 Privats.—The Massachusets Gives 1 Capt. 3 Subs 3 Serjts 2 Corpls & 80 Privaters — the Connecticutts Gives one Subn 1 Serjt 2 Corpls & 21 Privates.—N York 7 Privates. Rhod-Island 1 Serjt. 1 Corpl & 7 Privates.

The Capt. who is to Com.d ye Above Detachment to Wait on ye Commanding offr in Order to Receive His Instructions, this Evening at 6 oClock.—

Fort Edward July 27th 1757.

Parole *Fort-Wm.-Henry.*

The Detachment Order.d To March This Morning in Order to Relieve ye Detachment at Half Moon, To Strike their Tents By 1 oClock & Emmediately After to March to ye Island with their Tents and Camp Necessarys. & To Be In Readiness To March From thence as Soon as ye Waggon-Master Shall Have Provided them with proper Carriages.—

The Lines are Not to Turn out Upon any Alarm Till ye Proper Signals are Made of ye 23rd Instant.—And the Commanding offrs of ye Diferent Corps are To Se that these Orders are Strictly Comply.d with.—The offr Commanding ye Covering Party at ye Brick-kill is Emmediately upon Hearing any Shots in The Woods To Take Upon Him ye Com.d of the Workmen & File off Into ye Woods So Far as He May Judg Necessary in order To Get Upon ye Enimy's Rear & at ye Same Time To Send one Man of His Party To ye Commanding offrs To Acquaint Him of it.

The Ranging Companys To Be Under Arms this Evening at 6 oClock in Order to Be Review.d By the Commanding off.r—

Fort Edward July 28th 1757.
Parole *Hallyfax*
All ye Salers Ship Carpenters & Boatmen that Were Return.d By ye Several Corps To Hold them Selves in Readiness to March To ye Lake.—

Sd Detachment to Assemble on ye Grand Peraid Tomorrow Evening at Gun Firing In order to Be Review.d.—

The Ranging Companys Being to Fire at a Mark Between ye Hours of 4 & 6 oClock—The Troops To Be Emmediately Acquainted with it that They May Not Be Alarm.d with it.—In ye Same Time ye Commanding off.rs of ye Sevl Reg.ts May Send Such Men as Cannot Draw Their Charges to Fire them off In Presence of an Uncommission.d off.r. Who will Take Cair that their Men Fire Their Pieces Where No Accident May Happen.—

Fort Edward July 29th 1757
   Parole *Richmond.*

A Return To Be Given In Emmediately Signed By The Commanding off^r of Each Corps, of ye Ship Carpenters Salers & Boatmen that March.d This Morning To Fort W^m. Henry, And ye Reasons Why ye Compleat Number Was Not Sent as Return.d to Majr Morris.—

R. O. The Commanding off^r of Each Company in Gen^ll Lyman's Reg^t is Desired to Give in a Return Emmediately To ye Adj^t of ye Number Deficient of the Former Return & By What Reason.—

Fort Edward July 30th 1757.
   Parole *Radnorshire*

A Return To Be Given In Emmediately To ye Maj^r Brigaid of ye Number of off^rs Serj^ts. Corp^ls. & Private Men of Each Corp, Fit for Duty Mentioning those on Com.d at ye Different Posts Downwards & at Fort-William-Henry ye Several Persons Employ.d as Artificers Sailers & Boatmen in Each Corp are

Likewise To Be Included But are to Be Specify.d in a Different Colem by them Selves Mentioning ye Different Ranks of ye Different Persons & ye Perticular Plaices where they are Employ.d at.—

The off^rs Serj^ts Corp^ls & Private Men Upon Detachments are Likewise to Be Specify.d in Perticular Colems By them Selves.—This Return to Be Sign.d By ye Commanding off^r of Each Corp.—

Fort Edward July 31st 1757.
    Parole *Aberdeenshire.*
    If one Johnson of ye Connecticutt Reg^t Should Apply to Any other of ye Provencial Reg^ts For any Indians or Scoutes, they are to Be Emmediately Furnish.d to Him & ye Commanding off^r of ye Corp, To Acquaint ye Maj^r Brig-Aid of ye Number Sent.—

Fort Edward Augt 1st 1757
    Parole *Cavan.*
    Applycation is to Be Made to Mr Lesley For ye Number of Teems Requiset

To Carry ye Baggage of ye Troops To March Tomorrow—& the Gen^ll Desires that Non May Be Carry'd But What is Necessary, as It will Be Vary Dificult to Get Carriage to Bring it Down again.—

The Adj^t of the Massachusetts Reg^t To Send To ye Brigaid Maj^r ye Number of off^rs & Men on Duty Who are To March Tomorrow, that they May Be Rel.^d this Evening. — The Gen^ll Cort Mareschal Where of Col. Lyman Was President is Disolved. Lieut. Titcomb of the Massachusetts Reg^t, For Shamefully Quitting His Post, is Sentenced to Receive a Repremand of ye Gen^ll & therefor To Attend Him at 5 oClock this Afternoon in ye Fort.—

The Detachment of ye 60th Reg^t & Independant Companys that March Tomorrow Morning are Not To Take any Artifycers with them, That are Employ.d By the Inginear.—

Fort Edward Augt 2nd 1757.
    Parole *Kildare*

The Troops To Change their Present Encampment & Pitch their Tents on yᵉ Ground Alloted them By Mr. Lesley, & yᵉ New Ground to Be Cleaned Before yᵉ Men Pitch their Tents.—The Royˡ Americans & Connecticuts are To Strike their Tents First.—The Rest of yᵉ Troops To Be In Readiness to Strike when Mr. Lesley Informs them yᵉ Ground is Cleans.d.—

Fort Edward Augᵗ 3ʳᵈ· 1757
    Parole *Middlesex*

Fort Edward Augᵗ 4ᵗʰ 1757.
    Parole *Argileshire*
    A Return to Be Given in Emmediately of the Strength of Each Corp According To A Form which is To Be Given them By ye Majʳ Brig Aid.—This Return To Be Made as Exact as Possable.—
    The Guard in yᵉ Fort to be Mounted By yᵉ Ragular Troops Till Further Orders.—

R. O. The Commanding Off^r of Each Company In ye Connecticutt Reg^t are To Send in an Exact Return According To ye Above Order Emmediately to ye Adjt —To Be Don By a Form which He will Give them.—

The Men Ordered for Duty are allways To Appear With their Hats Cok.d & with Shoes & Stockings On Before they March to ye Grand Parade. And Any Serj^t or Corp^l that Marches their Men To ye Regimental Peraid to Se y^t Those Orders Are comply.d with.—

Fort Edward Augt 5th 1757.
    Parole *Dunbannonshire*
    The Lines To Turn out Tomorrow Morning at Gun Firing at ye Head of their Respective Incampments & there To Wate Till they Receive orders.—This To Be continued Till Countermanded.

Fort Edward Augt 6th 1757.
    Parole *Bumfree*
    Maj^r Prevost Field off^r of this Day

Fort Edward Augt 7th 1757.
  Parole *Edingborough*

Fort Edward Augt 8th 1757.
  Parole *Fifeshire*
  Maj^r Prevost Field off^r of ye Day Tomorrow.

The Troops To Have their arms & Ammunition Examened as Soon as Possable and Report To Be Made Emediately after to ye Gen^{ll} Signed by ye Commanding off^r of Each Corp., of ye Strength of their Respective Reg^{ts}, with Regard to ye Condition & Quantity of Ammunition & Number of Flints That Each Man Hath.—

The Gen^{ll} Expects y^t Capt^s & Commanding Off^{rs} of Companys will Be Vary Carefull in Viewing Their Men y^t this Return Ma Be as Exact as Possable.—

Fort Edward Augt 9th 1757.
  Parole Forfar
  R. O. That ye Commanding off^r of Each Company In ye Connecticutt Reg^t

Supply y[e] Deficiency of Powder Horns & Bullet Pouches with those Men's Accotrements y[t] are UnFit for Service.—This To Be Don Emediately & an Account of Such Powder Horns & Bullet Pouches To Be Taken that y[e] Right Owners Ma Not Loose them.

Fort Edward Aug[t] 10th 1757.

    Parole *Barwick*

A Return To Be Given in as Soon as Possable of The Number of Privates Belonging To Each Corp That are Come from Fort-Wm. Henry. Specifying those y[t] Have their Arms. This Return To Be Sign.d By y[e] Commanding off[r] of Each Reg[t.]

Fort Edward Aug[t] 11th 1757.

    Parole *Inverness*

A Return of y[e] Number of Persons that Hath Return.d from Fort-Wm. Henry Since Yesterday Morning Till To-Day at 12 oClock, Specifying Whether they Brought In any arms or Not. The

Same Return To Be Given In This Evening at Gun Firing And To Be Continued Every Forenoon & Evening Till Countermanded.

Fort Edward Augt 12th 1757.

    Parole *Newry*

    The off^{rs} & Men of ye 35th 60th & Independent Companys That are Return.d from Fort Wm. Henry To Peraid at Troop Beating In order To March To Albony.—The Commanding off^r of Each Corp To Make a Return of ye Number of Specifying Those y^t Have arms & Those y^t Have Not.—

Fort Edward Augt 13th 1757.

    Parole *Linlithgoo*

    The Field off^r of ye Day is Taken of, & ye Capt. of the Picq^t is To Visit ye Whol Picq^t once Every Hour From Retreat Beating Till Gun Firing in the Morning, To Se that they are Elert, & ye Capt: Is Every Morning To Report To Lord Howe the Hour He went

His Rounds, & To Acquaint Him of all Extraordinarys y^t May Happen in ye Night Time.—

For ye Future Upon any Alarm ye Ranging Companys are only To Turn out at ye Head of their Encampment. But they are Not To March out of ye Lines, Unless By an order from ye Gen^{ll} or Lord Howe.—

Fort Edward Augt 14th 1757.

Parole *Nairn*.

A return To Be Given in Emmediately To Mr. Lesley A. D. Q. M. G. of ye Number of Tents & Quantity of Baggage Belonging To ye Different Corps y^t is Left at Saratoge Still water & Half-Moon. & Each Corp is to Appoint a Proper Person To Go Down and Bring them Up.—This Return To Be Given in Emmediately to Mr. Lesley.

After Orders.—Whatsoever Centry Shall Be Found Mising when on Duty, or Sleeping on His Post, Shall Be Emmediately Confin.d & Shall Suffer Death.

—These Orders To Be Read To yᵉ Men By an Offʳ of a Company.

Fort Edward Augᵗ 15ᵗʰ 1757.
    Parole *Suffolk*

Fort Edward Augᵗ 16ᵗʰ
    Parole *Rippon*

Fort Edward Augᵗ 17ᵗʰ 1757.
    Parole *Wallingford*

The Genˡˡ Cort Mareschal Whereof Lord Howe was President is Disolv.d

A Return To Be Given as Soon as Possible of yᵉ Number of Men that are Deserted from Each Corp, Since yᵉ 11ᵗʰ Instᵗ· Specifying yᵉ Time They Have Ben Missing.

A Repᵗ To Be Made To yᵉ Majʳ Brig-Aid Every Morning at Troop Beeting of Those Men that were Missing yᵉ Evening Before at Roll Cal.—The Comm.dg offʳ of yᵉ Detachment yᵗ March.d to Saratoge to take under his

Charge ye French Deserters & Prisoners yt are here & from thence to Send them forward in ye Scow to Still water with a Searj^t. & 12 men where a Party from Albana will Receive them & conduct them there.—

After Orders. The Lines not to turn out again at Gun firing in ye Morning till further orders.—

Fort Edward Augt. 18th 1757.

Parole *Bedfordshire.*

Evening Ord. Whenever ye Commasary of Stors or Provisions Require any men to be Employ.d they are to Send their Demand in writing to ye Maj^r Brigaid at 11 oClock in ye Morning of ye Day before ye men are wanted Specifying ye number & for what Purpos they are wanting & without Such a Dem.d in Writing no man will be furnish.d them. And ye Commasarys to be answerable to Gen^ll Webb for any Delays in ye Kings Service Owing to their Neglect.

Fort Edward Aug. 19th 1757.

Parole *Boston*

The Ranging Companys, not ye Picqt to furnish ye Patroles in ye Night for ye future. Their Patroles will go out & Return through ye Barriers on ye Right & ye Barriers on ye Left of ye Camp. As soon as any Patroles Approach ye Camp, ye Sentrys will be Perticularly carefull in Challing & hail them & then to give notis to ye Officer of ye Piqt who will Send out a Searjt and file of men to Examin them before they Enter ye Camp.—

Tis Genll Lymans orders yt ye Commanding Offr of Each Company in his Regt give in as Soon as Possible, a Return of ye Names, & Plaices of Abode of all the Deserters & never joined & ye time when Deserted in Each Company.

Fort Edward Augt 20th 1757.

Parole *Sandwich*

Tis Genll Lymans orders, that no person in his Regt Shall Brew or Sell any fern Beer & whatsoever Person Shall Disobay this order Shall be Sevearly Punished.

Fort Edward Augt 21st 1757.
Parole *Barnstable*
No person whatsoever is to make use of any Boards Shingles or any other kind of timber yt is found in ye Camp with in ye Lines, or on ye ground where ye Milisha were Incamp.d without first Applying to Mr. Gordon Inginear—And if any one is found guilty of Disobaying these orders they will be very Sevearly Punished.—

R. O. That Murfa ye Gardiner hath ye whole cair of ye Connecticut Garden & no man to take any thing But of sd Murfa & by his order; & he to be Excused from all other Duty & Constantly to Attend on yt business.

That ye Commanding Offr of Each company in ye Connecticut Regt Sent in as Soon as possible to Genll Lyman a Duplicate Muster Role of their Companys, Specifying in Different Colems, y̅ᵉ time of Death, Desertion, Captivated Never joind &c., of their whole Companys Including yᵉ Number yᵉ Company first consisted off.—

The whole Regᵗ to turn out at Gun firing in yᵉ morning to call over yᵉ Role, & likewise at Evening. this order to be Strictly comply.d with.—

Fort Edward Augt 22ⁿᵈ 1757.
   Parole *Northampton*

Fort Edward Augᵗ 23ʳᵈ 1757.
   Parole *Litchfield*.
   G. O. The Genˡˡ Expects yᵗ his former orders forbidding yᵉ fireing of Pieses in, or near yᵉ Camp will be punctually comply.d with. All Commissiond & Non Commisⁿᵈ Offʳˢ are to confine Prisoner upon yᵉ next Guard any Person whom they Shall find Disobaying these Orders.—

Fort Edward Augt 24ᵗʰ 1757.
   Parole *Warwick*
   G. O. Whenever yᵉ weather will per-

mit ye Comm^{dg} Off^r of Each Corp are to order their mens tents to be Struck, ye Bark to be laid out in ye Street & ye Ground turn.d up.

Fort Edward Augt 25th 1757.
    Parole *York*.
    G. O. A Return to be given in as soon as possable of ye number of Sawyers in Each corp y^t are not Employ.d in ye Kings work.

Fort Edward Augt 26th 1757.
    Parole *Aldborrough*
    G. O. A Detachment of one Capt. 3 Sub^s 4 Searj^{ts} 4 Corp^{ls} & 96 men from ye Lines with one Capt. & 100 Rangers to peraid tomorow morning at Gun firing at ye Grand peraid to take their Blankets & 2 Days Provision with them.—The Eldest Capt. is to wait this Evening at Gunfiring on Lord Howe to receive his Instructions.

Fort Edward Augt 27th 1757.
    Parole *Salop*.

G. O. The Piq^t upon ye Right & Left of ye Camp to be Augmented with one Searjt. one Corp^l & 18 men Each till further orders.—Those Indians who were order.d some time ago to join Johnson belonging to ye Connecticut Troops are to Return to their Respective Corps again.

Fort Edward Augt 28th 1757.

Parole *Notingham.*

G. O. The Detachment y^t is in Fort-Edwd to furnish one Searj^t 1 Corp^l & 50 men Every Day to work in ye Fort They are to Assemble with ye other working partys on ye Grand Peraid.

Fort Edward Augt 29th 1757.

Parole *New-Port.*

G. O. Whoever is found Stealing Plank or timber belonging to ye Kings works will be Sevearly Punish.d Emediately — and ye Persons to whom ye hutts belong will be Responsible for it if any Such Timber is found in them.

GENERAL ORDERS OF 1757

The Detachment in ye Fort to march out this afternoon & to join their Respective Reg^{ts} in Camp, The Guards to mount tomorrow morning when they will be Relieved from ye Line.

After orders. A Gen^{ll} Cort-Mareschal consisting of one Field Off^r 4 Capt^s 2 Sub^s from ye Ragular Troops, & one Field Off^r 4 Capt^s & 1 Subⁿ from ye Provensials, to Set Tomorrow morning at 8 oClock at ye Presidents tent, or where he Shall Appoint.

Maj^r Fletcher President. Capt. Maunsel Judg Advocait

R. O. Majr Pason & Capt. Hitchcock for ye Court Mareschal.

Fort Edward Augt 30th 1757.

Parole *Staffordshire*.

G. O. No person to be Allowed to go hunt or kill game without a Pass Signed by ye Gen^{lls} A. D. Camp in which is to be Specifyd ye Number of ye Party & ye Reg^{ts} they belong too, & any person whatsoever not being on Duty who shall be protected [detected?] fireing his Pies within a mile of ye Camp will be order.d to receive 500 Lashes with a Cat of nine tales without a Court Mareschal.—The Commanding Offr of Each Reg^t to be answerable to Gen^ll Webb y^t there orders are comply'd with.

Fort Edward Augt 31st 1757.

Parole *Plymton*

G. O. When ever any Prisoners are confind upon Either of ye three Piq^ts, ye Off^r Commanding Such piq^ts is Emediately to send them to ye Fort Guard with their Crime in Writing & at ye Same time to Acquaint ye Commanding Off^r of ye Reg^t they belong too y^t Such men are Sent to ye Fort Guard from ye Piq^t.

R. O. Whereas it has been practised heatherto by Some of ye Commanding Off^rs of Companys in ye Connecticutt Reg^t to give in & Sign fals Returns, Tis Gen^ll Lymans orders y^t they take perticular cair for ye future as they will be Answerable for all such Neglects. & to prevent Such Mistakes Every Commissiond & Non Commissiond Off' in Each Company is Desired to keep a Muster Roll of their Companys & Enter ye time of death, Deserted, Discharged, Captivated & never joind of those men that are lost out of their Several Companys.

Fort Edward Septr 1st 1757.

    Parole *Bridgewater*.

    G. O. Coppy of ye Kings orders for ye Rank of Provensial Gen^lls & Field Off^rs in North-America, G. R.

    Whereas Some Disputes have Risen with Respect to ye Rank & comm^d which ye Gen^ll & Field Off^rs of ye Troops Raisd by ye Governors of our Provenses in N. America, should have when joind or Serving together with our Ragular forces in our s^d Provences, in order to fix ye Same & to prevent all Disputes on y^t Ac^t We Do hereby Declair y^t it is our will and Pleasure y^t all Gen^ll & Field Off^rs Serving by Commission from ye Governor, L^t or Deputy Governor or Presidents of yᵉ Counsel for yᵉ time being of our sᵈ Provences, Shall take Rank as Eldest Captˢ· on all Detachments Court Mareschals or other Duty wherein yᵉ sᵈ Genˡˡ or Field Offʳ may be Employed in N. America in Conjunction with our Ragular forces.— Given at our Court at Kensington yᵉ 12th Day of May 1756, in yᵉ 29th year of our Reign.

By his Majesties command. Henery Fox

R. O. Patt Welc Lately of ye 35th Regᵗ is appointed an Ensign in yᵉ 1ˢᵗ Company of yᵉ Connecticutt Regᵗ commanded by Phinehas Lyman Esqʳ and Standard bairer of yᵉ Same.

Fort Edward Sept.ʳ 2ⁿᵈ 1757.

Parole *Denvenshire.*

R. O. That all yᵉ men of from Duty in yᵉ Connecticutt Regᵗ in camp on this Side yᵉ River Rangers & all, Turn out at 3 oClock Every Afternoon to be Exercised till 5 By an Offʳ of yᵉ Regt who Shall be Appointed for yᵗ Porpose.

All ye Invaleades in ye Reg^ts to turn out at Such an hour as Doct^r Adams Shall Appoint in order to follow Doctr Odeas Directions & any of s^ds Invaleades y^t Refuse to comply with these orders Shall be Emmediately put upon Duty.—

Searj^t & Corp^ls to turn out their men to Attend Morning & Evening prayers which they are to Do as Soon as ye Drum beats for y^t porpose.

Fort Edward Sepr 3rd 1757.
Parole *Stanford*.

G. O. The Gen^ll Court mareschal whereof Maj^r Fletcher was President is Dissolved. Henery Dorman Corp^ll in Capt. Porters & Luelen Rice private Souldier in Capt. Delences Company, in ye Royal American Reg^t Having ben found Guilty of Desertion are Condamnd to Suffer Death for ye Same.

Frances Fleming private Souldier in ye Connecticut Reg^t having been found guilty of Desertion is Sentanced to Receive 1000 Lashes with a Cat of nine tails

& to be Drum'd out of ye Camp with a Holter about his neck.

Silley Hull, Wm. Mullen, John Jones, & Benjn Randal private Souldiers in ye N. York Reg^t Having been found guilty of Desertion are Sentenced to receive 1000 Lashes Each with a Cat of nine tails.

John Dun private Souldier in ye N. Jersey Reg^t being Tryed for Selling a Watch Coat belonging to ye 35th Reg^t is Ordered to Repay ye Several Sums he Rec^d for it & be Drum.d out of ye Camp with a Holter about his neck.

John Anderson private Souldier in ye Royal American Reg^t having been found Guilty of Mutiny is Sentenced to Receive 1000 Lashes with a Cat of nine tails.

The Gen^ll Having Approved of ye above Sentences, They are to be put in Execution on Monday morning next at 8 oClock.

Roger Connolly private Souldier in ye Massachusetts Reg^t being found guilty of mutiny, is orderd to Receive 500 Lashes with a Cat of nine tails.

John Rider private Souldier in ye N. York Reg^t being tried for Sleeping on his post is found guilty & is Sentanced to Receive 500 Lashes with a Cat of nine tails.

Peter Thear private Souldier in ye Massachusetts Reg^t being found Guilty of Desertion is Sentanced to Receive 500 Lashes with a Cat of nine tails.

The Gen^ll has been pleas.d to pardon John Rider, Roger Connolly & Peter Thear. They are to be Emmediately Sent for from ye Guard to their Respective Reg^ts.

As it appears y^t through Neglect of Off^rs ye Articles of war have never been Read to Several of ye Souldiers in ye Provencial Troops, Tis therefore Gen^ll Webb's order y^t ye Commanding Off^rs of Each Reg^t Do Assemble their respective Companys & after having read ye Articles of War Cause Each man present to Sign a paper which ye Capt. or Comm^dg Off^r of ye Comp^y is Likewise to Sign as witnesses y^t they were Present at ye Reading of them.—

GENERAL ORDERS OF 1757

Fort Edward Sept. 4th 1757.

Parole *Pembrook*

G. O. A Detachment of 10 men of a Comp^y from ye Line with one Capt. 2 Subs. 2 Searj^ts, 2 Corp^ls to Every 50 men & one Field Off^r to Com^d ye Whole to peraid tomorrow morning at ye Grand peraid at 7 oClock in order to Attend ye Execution of Corp^ll Dorman & Lualen Rice of ye Royal Amarican Reg^t who are to be Shot by a Plattoon of ye Companys they belong too.—The Royal American Reg^t to Send one Sub^n 1 Searjt 1 Corp^l & 24 men to bring ye Prisoners to ye Plais of Execution.—Maj^r Fletcher to Com^d ye Party for ye Execution.

The commander at Saratoge to be Relieved on Tuesday Morning next.

R. O. That Capt. Jeffery with 3 of his Sub^ns 2 Searj^ts 2 Corp^ls & 60 men Attend ye Execution & to be Ready on ye Peraid at 7 oClock tomorrow morning & ye men to Appear Clean & in a Deasant manner. Capt. Whittlecy & Lieu^t Castle for ye above com^d.

Fort Edward Septr ye 5th 1757.

Parole *Durham*.

The Commanding Off^{rs} of ye Different Corps are to Order a Party Every morning to Clear ye Ground without ye Lines along ye Front of their Respective Regt^s, all Filth & Nastiness is to be taken away. —The Com^{dg} Off^{rs} to be answerable to ye Gen^{ll} y^t these orders are Complyd. with

Fort Edward Septr 6th 1757

Parole *London*

Fort Edward Sept. 7th 1757.

Parole *Plymmouth*.

G. O. The Sentrys are not to Suffer any Person to go out at ye Barriers in ye Front of ye Camp after Dark.

Fort Edward Septr ye 8th 1757.

Parole *Newtown*.

Fort Edward Septr ye 9th 1757.

Parole *Glosester*.

GENERAL ORDERS OF 1757

Fort Edward Sept. ye 10th 1757.
   Parole *Glasgow*

Fort Edward Septr 11th 1757.
   Parole *Woodstock*

Fort Edward Septr 12th 1757.
   Parole *Monmoth*

Fort Edward Septr 13th 1757.
   Parole *Anglesea.*

G. O. The men of ye Different Corps y^t are with ye Artilery are to join & Do Duty with their Respective Reg^ts.

Capt. Wests Comp^y of Rangers to be compleated from Capt. Larnards & ye Remainder of Capt. Larnards men after Capt. Wests Comp^y is Compleated to do Duty with ye Massachusetts on ye Island. Capt. Jefferys & Capt. Walls Companys are to join their Corps & to do Duty in ye Line.—

A Gen^ll Court Mareschal to Consist of one Field Off^r Six Capt^s Six Sub^s to set tomorrow morning at 8 oClock at ye Presidents Tent. Maj^r Prevo President.—

R. O. That Capt. Jefferys make a Return to ye Adjutant as Soon as possable of ye Number of Off^{rs} & men fit & unfit for Duty in his Ranging Company y^t join ye Reg^t —Searj^t Nott is Likewise to give in a Return of his men.

Fort Edward Septr ye 14th 1757
    Parole *Thetford*

G. O. A Capt. 2 Sub^{s.} 4 Searj^{ts} 4 Corp^{lls} & 96 men of ye Provensials to hold them Selves in Readiness to March tomorrow morning to Stillwaters.—The commanding Off^{rs} to Receive his orders this Evening at Gunfiring of Capt. Bartman Aid De Camp to Gen^{ll} Webb.

Fort Edward Sept. ye 15th 1757.
    Parole *Bristol*

Fort Edward Sept. 16th 1757.
    Parole *Saram*

G. O. All ye Provensial Troops are Emmediately to move out of ye Camp & onto ye Island where they will pitch their Tents in ye most convenient manner till ye Ground is Cleard.—The Quarter master & Quarter Searj^t to apply to M^r. Lesley this afternoon who will Shew them the Ground their Respective Reg^ts are to Encamp on.—

The Provensial Reg^ts to furnish their proporsion of Off^rs & men for ye Piq^t till further Orders & by turns to furnish an Adjutant of ye Day to peraid all Partys y^t may be orderd from ye Island & also to attend ye Maj^rs Brigaid for ye orders of ye Day. The Provensial Troops are to be under Com^d of Col. Lyman who is to Send a Report in Writing Every Day to ye Gen^ll by ye Adjutant of ye Day & all Extraordinarys to be Reported Emediately.

Fort Edward Septr ye 17th 1757
    Parole *Malmsberry*.
    G. O. Field Off^r for tomorrow Maj^r Marsey.

All Persons Guilty of crimes Cognasable for a Regimental Court Mareschal are to be confind by ye Quarter Guard of ye Reg^t they belong to, & those for Capital Crimes to be Sent to ye Fort Guard.

The Parole is to be sent to ye Field Offr of ye Day in writing by ye Majr Brigaid.

The Adj^t of ye 17th & 27th Reg^ts to get Standing orders of ye Maj^r Brigaid.

Gen^ll Webb not approving of Several of ye Sentences of ye Gen^ll Court Mareschal whereof Maj^r Prevo is President, they are to meet again tomorrow morning at 9 oClock at ye Presidents Tent in order to revise them.

R. O. Searj^ts David Pike of Gen^ll Lymans Company Being Tryed by a Regimental Court mareschal for Neglect of Duty is Reduced to ye Ranks & to Do Duty as Such.

Fort Edward Sept 18th 1757.

Parole *Londendary*.

G. O. Field Off^r for tomorrow. Maj^r Prevo.

Fort Edward Septr 19th 1757.

Parole *Westbury*.

G. O. Field Off^r for tomorrow Maj^r Fletcher.

Adj^t for ye Rag^{ls} ye 35th Reg^r.—For ye Provensials ye N.-York Reg^t.

The 17th & Inneskilling Reg^{ts} to give in a Return as Soon as Possable of their Carpenters, Ship Carpenters, Sawyers, Brick layers, & Joiners y^t are in Each of their Corps.

Whenever any Reg^t has occasion to Send any men over to ye Island they are to Send a Non Commissiond Off^r with them & if any men want to go over after their own Business they are to have a pass in writing Signed By ye Capt. or Com^{dg} Off^r of ye Compy they belong too which is to be Returnd back when they Return. And ye Com^{dg} Off^r of ye Provensial Troops on ye Island is to Send back all Souldiers belonging to ye Ragulars, Prisoners to their Respective Reg^{ts} who Shall be found on ye Island not having a Pass without a Non Comm^d Off^r with them—

Any Souldier found Guilty of Disobaying this Order Shall be Sevearly punished.

Orders for Ragulating ye Duty of ye Provensials on ye Island.

The Guard to consist of one Capt. 2 Sub^s· 8 Searj^{ts} 8 Corp^{ls} & 80 men who are to mount at Troop beating in ye morning Every Day. out of which Number there is one Searj^t one Corp^{ll} & 9 men to be sent from ye Grand Peraid to Each Corp as a Quarter Guard. The Searjt^s are to make their Reports to ye Capt. of ye Main Guard Before they are Relieved & ye Capt. to ye Com^{dg} Off^r of ye Provensials. The Sentrys to be Reliev.d Every 2 hours in ye Day time & once Every hour in ye Night. After Tattoe a Searj^t or Corp^{ll} with a file of men to Patrole betweend Every Relief & a Sub^m to go ye Rounds at 12 oClock & another at 2 & ye Capt. to go ye Grand Rounds at 3 oClock to Se y^t ye Sentrys are Elert & Watchfull on their posts.

R. O. Searj^t Dickinson of Capt. Jefferys Company in ye Connecticutt Reg^t is

Reduced to ye Ranks & to Do Duty as Such. And Corp. David Handee of s^d Company is appointed Searj^t in s^d Dickinsons Room & to be obeyd as Such.

Fort Edward Sept. 20th 1757.
    Parole *Montgomery*
    G. O. Field Off^r for tomorrow Lt Col. Morris.
Adj^t for ye Ragulars ye 60th Regt.—For ye Provensials ye Massachusetts Reg^t.
    Gen^{ll} Webb being Informed Last night there was a grate Noise & Disturbance of ye Ragularity of ye Several parts of ye Camp Hoping y^t for ye Future he Shall not be Obliged to give out Orders which will be Equally Disagreeable with himself as to ye Persons Guilty.
    Capt. Thody of ye N. York Reg^t is to Attend ye Different Corps whenever ye Post comes from Albany & Each Reg^t is to Send a Proper Person to Receive ye Letters & ye Person to pay ye postage Due for Such Letters as are Demanded by ye postmaster at Albany,

otherwise they will not be Delivered them.

The Drum^{rs} are not to be allowd to practise before Troop Beating in ye Mornings.

Gen^{ll} Lymans Orders. The Quarter Masters of Each Regt Emediately to See that there are Necessary houses Dug about 100 Yards Advainsed in ye Front of ye Incampment which are to be coverd over Every Day with Dirt & when about half full they are to be fild up & Newones Dug.—

That ye Quartermaster of ye Massachusetts Se yt ye Bank on ye East of ye Island be made & kept clean & ye Quarter Master of ye Connecticutt to Do ye Same on ye West Bank & y^t Quarter Master Ripley takes cair to Build a Necessary house over ye River below ye Off^{rs} Tents for ye Use of ye Off^{rs}.

That ye Field Off^{rs} be Field Off^{rs} of ye Day by turns Day about & ye Capt^s of ye Guards to make their Returns to them & they to ye Comman^{dg} Off^r as Soon as

GENERAL ORDERS OF 1757

Convenient after ye Relief of ye Guard in ye morning.
Coll: Glayser Field Off^r of this Day.

Fort Edward Septr 21st 1747.
    Parole *Minchead*.
G. O. Field Off^r Tomorrow Maj^r Prevo. Adj^t for ye Ragu^ls ye Independ^t Companys Adj^t for ye Provensials ye Connecticutts.

    Two Companys of ye Inniskilling Reg^t will Peraid tomorrow morning at 7 oClock.

    A Patrole consisting of a Corp^l & 2 men at Tattoe beating in ye Fort to visit ye Hutts with out ye Lines & to confine all Souldiers to be found in them.

    All Off^rs are Desired to confine any man y^t they find Gaming & to Send them Prisoners to ye Fort Guard.

    The Piq^t & Guard for ye Future to lode with ye havy ball & ye Command^g off^rs of Corps are to Apply to ye Train for ye Quantity of Cors powder they will want.

The Gen^ll Court Mareschal whereof Maj^r Prevo was Presid^t is Disolved.

A Gen^ll Court Mareschal to consist of one Field Off^r Six Capt^s & Six Sub^s of ye Ragular Troops to Set tomorrow morning at ye Presidants tent.

Lieut. Coll: Haviland Presidant. Capt: Charters Judge Advocait.

Fort Edward Sepr 22nd 1757.
    Parole *Truro.*
G. O. Field Off^r for tomorrow Maj^r Darby.
    Adj^t for ye Ragulars ye 17th Reg^t. Adj^t for ye Provencials ye N. York Reg^t.
    Field Offr for ye Provencials Coll. Glayser.

Fort Edward Sept 23rd 1757.
    Parole *Penryn.*
    G. O. Field Off^r for tomorrow Lieut. Col. Haviland
    Adj^t for ye Ragulars ye Inniskilling Reg^t. Adj^t for ye Provensials ye Rhod Island Regt.

Field Offr for ye Provensial Col. Angel.

The Genll Court Mareschal whereof Lieut. Col. Haviland is President is Dissolv.d & ye Genll Having Approv.d of ye Sentance of Joseph Coser, Corp^l of Capt. Porters Company in ye Royal American Reg^t having ben Tryed for being Insolent to Searjt Mackinsey of s^d Company & Reg^t & Knocking him Down, is acquitd.

For ye future Commissiond & Non Commd Off^{rs} Comm^{dg} Guards are to Send a man of their Guard to ye Adj^t of ye Reg^t they belong too for ye Parole, who is to Send it in writing Signd.

Fort Edward Septr ye 24th 1757.

Parole *Worcester*.

G. O. Field Off^r for tomorrow, Majr Marsa

Adj^t for ye Ragulars ye 35th Reg^t. Adj^t for ye Provensials ye Massachusetts Reg^r. Field Offr for ye Provensials Maj^r Pason.

R. O. Capt. Fitch for Guard tomorrow.

Corpl Jacob Andrus of Capt: Fitchs company is appointed Serj^t in s^d company & is to be obeyd. as Such.—

Gideon Dike & James Cobb are appointed Corp^{lls} in s^d Company & are to be obeyed as Such.—

Fort Edward Sept. 25th 1757.

Parole *Gatton.*

G. O. Field Of^r for tomorrow Maj^r Fletcher.

Adj^t for y^e Rag^{ls} y^e 60th Reg^t for y^e Provensials y^e Connecticutt Reg^t Field off^r for y^e Provensials Col Glayser.

Three companys of y^e 17th Reg^t will fire tomorrow morning at 7 oClock.

Fort Edward Sept. 26th 1757.

Parole *Hartford.*

G. O. Field Offr for tomorrow L$^{t.}$ Col. Morris.

Adj^t for y^e Rag^{ls} y^e Independants.

for y^e Provencials y^e N. Yorke Reg^t Field Off^r for y^e Provensials Col. Angel.

The Capt. Guard on y^e left of y^e lines to be Augmented Every Evening with two Corp^{lls} & 12 men who are to peraid at y^e Same time of y^e, Piq^t.

Fort Edward Septr 27th 1757.

Parole *Ludlow*.

G. O. Field Off^r for tomorrow Maj^r Prevo

Adj^t for ye Rag^{ls} ye 17th Reg^t. Adj^t for ye Provensials ye Rhod-Island Reg^t.

Field Off^r for ye Provensials Maj^r Pason.

The Corps of Lieu^t Harrison to be Buried tomorrow morning at 8 oClock & a Lieu^{ts} Com^d from ye Ragulars to Attend his burial.

Fort Edward Sept. 28th 1757.

Parole *Shoreham*.

G. O. Field Offr for tomorrow Maj^r Darby

Adjt for ye Ragulars ye Inniskilling

Reg.t Adj.t for y.e Provensials & Massachusetts Reg.t

Col. Glayser Field Off.r for y.e Provensials.

No body to fire at mark but by leave & only between y.e hour of 10 & 12 oClock in y.e forenoon, & all y.e Targaits to be put up in Front of y.e Grand Peraid & no where Else.

R. O. Capt. Whittlecy & Ens.n Tracy for Guard tomorrow.

Fort Edward Sept. 29.th 1757.

Parole *Shaftsbury.*

G. O. Field off.r for tomorrow L.t Col. Haviland.

Adjt for y.e Rag.ls y.e 35th Regt. Adj.t for y.e Provensials y.e Connecticutt Reg.t

Field Off.r for y.e Provensials Col. Angel.

Tis Gen.ll Lymans orders that y.e off.rs belonging to y.e Provensial Troops on y.e Island, Incamp in their Respective plaises in y.e Rear of their Reg.ts

When ever any Fireing is heard in

ye Woods ye Capt. of ye Main Guard is to Send a Searjt & 12 men to Fetch in ye Persons Fireing & confine them to ye Main Guard.

No Person is to go a hunting with out leave from Capt. Bartman Gen^{ll} Webb's A. D. Camp, & then not to fire within a mile of ye Camp.

Ens^n Baldwain for Guard tomorow. Ensn Minor for ye Saratoge Com^d.

Fort Edward Septr 30th 1757.

Parole *Rutland*.

G. O. Field Offr for tomorrow Maj^r Marsa.

Adjt for ye Rag^{ls} ye 60th Reg^t Adj^t for ye Provensials ye Rhod Island Reg^t.

Field offr for ye provensials Majr Pason.

R. O. Lt John Durke for guard tomorrow.—

Fort Edward Oct. 1st 1757.

Parole *Surrey*.

GENERAL ORDERS OF 1757

G. O. Field Off^r for tomorrow Maj^r Fletcher.

Adj^t for ye Ragu^ls ye Indep^t Comp^ys. Adj^t for ye Provensials ye N. York Reg^t.—

Field Off^r for ye Provensials Col. Glayser.

Fort Edward Oct. 2nd 1757.

Parole *Cornwall.*

G. O. Field Off^r for tomorow Lt Col: Morris.

Adj^t for ye Rag^ls ye 17th Reg^t. Adj^t for ye Provensials ye Massachusetts Reg^t.

Field Off^r for ye Provensials Col. Angel.

Gen^ll Webb having Approved of ye Sentance of ye Gen^ll Court Mareschal where of Lord Howe was Presid^t which is as follows.

Lieu^t Noles of ye Massachusetts Reg^t having Ben Tried for Saying in ye hearing of Capt. West of s^d Reg^t & others that there is no man at Fort Edward or in this Camp that hath Power to Com^d ye Massachusetts Souldiers to Stay here & if they go home nobody can punish them.—It is ye Opinion of this Court Mareschal y^t ye s^d Lt Noles is guilty of ye Accusation laid to his charge & comes under the Breach of ye 3rd Article of ye 2nd Sect : of ye Articles of War and therefore Do Adjudge y^t afors^d Lt Noles have his Sword Break over his Head at ye Head of ye Afors^d Reg^t and to be Banish.d out of ye Camp & Dismissd from his Majestys Service.

It is therefore ye Gen^lls orders y^t s^d Sentence be put in Execution tomorrow morning at 8 oClock at ye head of ye Provensial Camp. at which time a Piq^t consisting of one Capt. 2 Sub^s 2 Searj^ts. 2 Corp^ls & 48 men from Each of ye Provensial Reg^ts to be under arms & to Attend.

R. O. Lieu^t Simons for Guard tomorow.

Fort Edward Oct. 3rd 1757.
    Parole *Malden*.

G. O. Field Off^r for tomorow Maj^r Prevo.

Adj^t for ye Ragulars ye Inniskilling Reg^t. Adj^t for ye Provensials ye Connecticutt Reg^t.

Field Off^r for ye Provensials Maj^r Pason.

A Detachment of two Capt^s Six Sub^s 7 Searj^{ts} 8 Corp^{ls} & 192 men to Peraid tomorrow morning at Gun firing with Arms. M^r. Lesley A. D. Q. M. Gen^{ll} will give them their directions. they are to be Relieved by ye like number of Off^{rs} & men at 12 oClock who are to Remain upon y^t work till Evening & ye Off^{rs} are to be allowed only a Piq^t Duty in ye Gen^{ll} Roster.—The Provensial Troops are Likewise to Peraid tomorow morning on ye Island at ye Same time one Sub: 2 Searj^{ts}. 2 Corp^{ls} & 50 men with arms who are to be provided with falling Axes. y^t Party is likewise to receive their Directions from M^r. Lesley.

As Soon as ye Adj^{ts} have got ye Detail of ye Number y^t Each of their Corps are to furnish, they are to Acquaint their Quarter Master Searj^{ts} who are to apply this afternoon to M^r. Lesley for Tools which are to be DD out to them upon their Regimental Peraid tomorow morning.

Gen^{ll} Lymans orders. That all ye Falling Axes in Each of ye Provensial Reg^{rs} be Emediately Returnd to ye Comdg Offrs of Regts who are to appoint some person as they Shall think Sutable to se y^t they are all Ground up & prepaired for Service & to Detach a Sutable number of men for that porpose & all Persons y^t have any Axes in their possession & Do not Return them as above are to be Punishd as Embaslers of ye Kings stors.   P. Lyman

R. O. The Comm^{dg} off^r of Each Comp^y in ye Connecticutt Reg^t are forthwith to give in a Muster Roll of their Companys Specifying in Diferent Colems those y^t are Dead by Sickness, Kild by ye Enimy, Captivated, Deserted, Never joind, with ye Day of ye Month.

By ye Gen^{lls} order Timothy Hierlihy Adjutant.

Fort Edward Oct* 4th 1757.

Parole *Janworth*.

G. O. Field Off* for tomorow Maj* Darbe

Adjt for yᵉ Ragulars yᵉ 35th Reg*· Adjᵗ for yᵉ Provensials yᵉ N. York Reg*·

Field Off* for ye Provensials Col: Glayser.

The Same number of Off*ˢ & men as in Yesterdays orders & to be Relieved in yᵉ Same manner.—

R. O. All yᵉ Commissiond off*ˢ of from Duty in yᵉ Connecticut Regᵗ to turn out Every morning at Such an hour as Ensⁿ Welch Shall Appoint for Exercise & the privates in yᵉ Afternoon for that purpose.

Fort Edward Oct* 5th 1757.

Parole *Lymington*

G. O. Field Offr for tomorrow Lᵗ Col: Haviland.

Adjᵗ for yᵉ Ragulars yᵉ 60th Reg*·

Adj^t for y^e Provensials y^e Rhodisland Reg$^{t.}$

Field Offr for y^e Provensials Col. Angel.

The working partys to be continu.d & to be Relieved as this Day till further Orders.

R. O. Capt: Hitchcock & Lt Billings for Guard Tomorrow.

Fort Edward Octr 6th 1757.

Parole *Aar*.

G. O. Field Off^r for tomorrow Lt Col: Morris.

Adjt for y^e Rag^{ls} y^e Indipandant Companys. Adj^t for y^e Provensials y^e Massachusetts Reg$^{t.}$

Field Offr for y^e Provensials Maj^r Pason.

Fort Edward Octr 7th 1757.

Parole *Sussex*.

G. O. Field Off^r for tomorrow Maj^r Prevo.

Adj^t. for y^e Rag^{ls} y^e 17th Reg^t Adj^t for y^e Provens^{ls} y^e Connect^s

Field Off^r for y^e Provensials Col: Glayser

R: O: Capt: Fitch & Ens^n Parsons for Guard Tomorrow.

Fort Edward Octr 8th 1757.

Parole *Rochesterfield.*

G. O. Field Off^r for tomorrow Maj^r Derba.

Adj^t for ye Rag^{ls} ye Inniskilling Reg^t. Adj^t for ye Provensials ye N. York Reg^t.

Field Off^r for ye Provensials Col: Angel

Capt Wests Company of Rangers to return to their respective Companys & to do Duty there.

Tis Gen^{ll} Lymans orders that ye Comm^{dg} Off^r of Each of ye Provensial Reg^{ts} Se that there is a Peraid made in ye Front of their Encampment & y^t all ye Streets & Allies in ye camp are kept clean.

Capt: Wests Ranging company Emmediately to Strike their Tents & Pitch with ye Reg^t of their Reg^t.—

R. O. David Pike of Gen^ll Lymans & Charles Ripley of Capt: Slaps Companys are Restored to Searj^ts & to be Obay.d as Such.—

Fort Edward Octr 9th 1757.
 Parole *Cambridge.*
 G. O. Field Off^r for tomorrow Maj^r Fletcher.
 Adj^t for ye Rag^ls ye 35th Reg^t. Adj^t for ye Provens^ls ye Rhod Island Reg^t.
 Field Off^r for ye Provensials Maj^r Pason.
 R. O. That ye Off^rs of ye Several Companys in ye Connecticut Reg^t are to take Spatial cair y^t ye men of their Several Companys build their Chimnys in Such a manner as will best Secure ye mens Helth, Prevent Damage in their Tents and Cloths & make ye most Deasent and Souldierlike Appearence that is Possable.

Fort Edward Octr 10th 1757.

Parole *Wendover.*

G. O. Field offr for Tomorow Lt Col. Morris.

Adj^t for ye Rag^{ls} ye 60th Reg^t Adj^t for ye Provensials ye Massachusetts Regt Field off^r for ye Prov^{nls} Col : Glayser.

The Provensial Troops are to Send over this afternoon at 4 oClock to Mr. Euings Cleark of Ordnance Stores all the Axes they have Rec^d Except ye 60 Now Employd By ye working partys on ye Hill.—The commanding Off^{rs} of Different Corps to be answerable to Gen^{ll} Webb that this order is strictly Obayd.

The Effects of ye Late Lt Harrison of ye Royal Artilery to be Disposed off by Publick Oction Tomorow in the Afternoon in ye Rear of ye Artilery Park.

Fort Edward Octr 11th 1757.

Parole *Ducksbury.*

G. O. Field off^r for tomorow Maj^r Prevo.

Adj^t for ye Rag^{ls} ye Independants.—

GENERAL ORDERS OF 1757

Adj^{ts} for the Provensials ye Connecticutts.

Field Off^r for ye Provensials Col. Angel.

A Court of Enquiery Consisting of Col. Lyman Col. Glayser. Col. Angel Maj^r Pason & Capt; Carver of ye Massachusetts Regt Set tomorow morning at 7 oClock at Col: Lymans Tent to Examen into ye Complaint of Lt Russel of ye Rhodisland Reg^t against Capt. Wall of S^d Reg^t & give in their Opinion to Gen^{ll} Webb.

Fort Edward Octr 12th 1757.

Parole *Sarum*

G. O. Field Off^r for tomorow Maj^r Darbe

Adj^t for ye Rag^{ls} ye 17th Reg^t. Adj^t for ye Provensials ye N. York Reg^t.

Field Offr for ye Provensials Maj^r Pason.

The Troops to Receive 4 Days Salt & 3 Days Fresh Provision Till farther orders.

The working party Employd on ye Hill are for ye Future to peraid at 7 oClock Every morning & not to Retn till Evening. ye men are to carry their Provision for ye Day with them.

R. O. Capt: Jeffery For Guard tomorow.—Ensn Baldwain for Saratoge.

Fort Edward Octr 13th 1757.

Parole Nairn.

G. O. Field Offr for tomorow Majr Fletcher.

Adjt for ye Ragls ye Inniskilling Regt. Adjt for the provensials ye Rhod Island Regt.

Field Offr for ye Provensials Col: Glayser.

Fort Edward Octr 14th 1757.

Parole *Inverness*

G. O. Field Offr for tomorow Lt Col: Morris

Adjt for ye Ragls ye 35th Regt. Adjt for ye Provencials ye Massachusetts Regiment.

GENERAL ORDERS OF 1757

Field Off^r for y^e Provensials Col: Angel.

The Field Off^r of y^e Day to make his Report to the Eldest Field Off^r in Camp.—

Agreable to Gen^{ll} Webbs order to us to Enquire into ye Complaint of Lieu^t Russel of y^e Rhod Island Reg^t against Capt. Wall of s^d Reg$^{t.}$ We have persuant to that Carefully Examen.d into y^e affair & it is our Oppinion y^e Capt: Wall is guilty of y^e Crime Exhibited by Lt Russel as he can Soport it by a number of Witnesses. And it is our further Oppinion y^t Capt: Wall ask Lt. Russels Pardon at y^e head of y^e Reg^t before y^e Col: & all his Off$^{rs.}$

    P. Lyman
    B. Glayser
    S. Angel
    N. Pason
    J. Carver

Orders That Capt. Wall ask Lt Russels pardon at y^e head of y^e Rhod Island

Regt according to ye above Sentence of ye Court of Enquiery.

Fort Edward Octr 15th 1757
    Parole *Glasgow.*
    G. O. Field Off^r for tomorow Maj^r· Prevo.
    Adj^t for y^e Rag^{ls} y^e Royal Amarican Reg$^{t.}$—Adj^t for the Provensials y^e Connecticut Reg$^{t.}$
    Field Off^r for y^e Provensials Maj^r Pason.
    Gen^{ll} Lymans orders. That no person is allowed to play with Panies in ye Provensial Camp & whatever person Disobays these orders will be Severaly Punish.d

Fort Edward Octr 16th 1757.
    Parole *Barwick.*
    G. O. Field Off^r for tomorow Maj^r Darbe.
    Adj^t for y^e Rag^{ls} y^e Indipendant Company. Adj^t for the Provensials y^e N. York Reg$^{t.}$

Field Off^r for y^e Provensials Col: Glayser

Fort Edward Octr 17th 1757.
Parole *Argyle*
G. O. Field Off^r for tomorow Maj^r Fletcher.
Adjt for y^e Rag^lls y^e 17th Reg^t. —Adj^t for y^e Provensials y^e Rhod-Island Reg^t.
Field Off^r for ye Provensials Col: Angel.
The Several Reg^ts & Independant Companys now at Fort Edward Emediately to prepair Muster Rolls from ye 25th of April 1757 to ye 24th of Octr following. Each Comp^y to have one parchment & Four paper Rolls.
R. O. Each Company of ye Connecticut Reg^t is Emediately to give in to ye Adj^t ye names of those y^t have Died, Deserted, Discharged, &c. in their Several Companys Since ye 3rd of Octr Inst.—
Searj^t Josiah Smith of Captt: Slapps Company is by Gen^ll Lymans order Redused to ye Ranks & to Do Duty as Such

for unfaithfulness in his Duty when on Guard.

Capt: Wells & Lt Fitch for Guard tomorow.

Fort Edward Octr 18th 1757.

Parole *Sterling*.

G. O. Field Off^r for tomorow Lt Col: Morris.

Adj^t for y^e Rag^{ls} y^e y^e Inniskilling Reg^t.—Adj^t for y^e Provensials y^e Massachusetts Reg^t

Field Off^r for ye Prov$^{nls.}$ Maj^r Pason.

The Pioniers & Camp Colermen of Each Company with a Quarter Master Searj^t from Each Corp to peraid tomorrow morning Emediately after Guard mounting with their Tools in order to build Hutts for y^e Several Guards in y^e Lines The whole to be under y^e Direction of y^e Quarter Master of ye 17th Reg^t. who is to Receive his orders from ye Field Off^r of ye Day.

N. B. The men for work are to bring

their Breakfast with them as they will not be allowd to go to ye Island till Din^r.

R. O. Capt: Hitchcock & Lt Huntly for Guard tomorow

Fort Edward Octr 19th 1757.
Parole *Cliston*
G. O. Field Off^r for tomorow Maj^r Prevo.

Adj^t for ye Rag^ls ye 35th Reg^t.— Adj^t for ye Prov^sls the Connecticutt Reg^t.

Field Off^r for ye prov.^sls Col. Glayser.

John Rhodes a private Souldier in ye Royal Amarican Reg^t having ben Tried at a Gen^ll Court-Mareschal for Stealing Several Species of Goods (ye property of Garshom Levi) is found guilty of ye charge layd against him & is Sentanc.d to Suffer Death for ye Same.

Fraderic Young a private Souldier in ye Royal Amarican Reg^t having ben Tried at a Gen^ll Court Mareschal for Stealing Sundry Species of Goods (ye property of Garshom Levi) is found guilty of ye Theft Laid to his charge and is Sentanced to

Receive 1000 Lashes with a Cat of 9 tails & to be Drumd out of ye Reg^t with a Holter about his Neck & with a Labell upon his Brest.

George Leynord a private Souldier in ye Royal Amarican Reg^t having ben Tried at a Gen^ll Court Mareschal for Stealing Sundry Species of goods (ye property of Gershom Levi) is found guilty of ye Theft Laid to his charge & is Sentenced to receive 1000 Lashes with a cat of 9 tails and to be Drumd out of ye Reg^t with a Holter about his Neck & with a Labill upon his Brest.

John Kim a private Souldier in ye Royal Amarican Reg^t having ben Tryed at a Gen^ll Court Mareschal for Stealing Sundry Species of goods (ye property of Garshom Levi) is found Guilty of ye Theft Laid to his charge & is Sentanced to Receive 500 Lashes with a cat of 9 tails.

Andrew Westerman a private Souldier in ye Royal Amarican Reg^t having ben Tried at a Gen^ll Court Mareschal for Desertion & also for Stealing Sundry Species of goods (ye property of Garshom Levi) is found guilty of ye whole charge layd against him & is Sentanced to Suffer Death for ye Same.

John McDuffy a private Souldier in ye N. York Reg{t} Having ben tryed at a Genll Court Mareschall for Deserting & Stealing Capt: Bellew's horse of ye 35th Reg{t} is found guilty of ye Charge brought against him & is Sentanced to Suffer Death for ye Same.

The Genll Having approved of ye above Sentances is pleasd to order that John Rhodes & John Westerman private Souldiers in ye Royal American Reg{ts} Do Suffer Death tomorow morning at 8 oClock.—John McDuffy private Souldier in ye N. York Reg{t} be Pardon.d.

The Field Off{r} of ye Day with ye Piq{t} of ye Line, & a Detachment of One Capt: 2 Sub{s.} 2 Searj{ts.} 2 Corp{lls} & 48 men from N. York Reg{t} to Attend ye Execution.

As Soon as ye Piq{t} is formd ye Field

Off.r of ye Day is to order a Searj.t & 12 men with ye Prevos to go & fetch the Prisoners. John McDuffy & ye other Prisoners orderd to receive Corpl Punishment are likewise to march to ye plais to attend ye Execution.

The Troop not to beet tomorow morning till 10 oClock & ye Guards to Peraid Emediately after.

The Prevo is to take cair to have Labills fixt upon the Brests of ye Prisoner ordered to Suffer Death Specifying the Crimes for which they Suffer.

R. O. L.t Harden for Guard tomorow.

Fort Edward Oct.r 20th 1757.

Parole *Wenchester.*

G. O. Field Off.r tomorow Maj.r Darbe.

Adj.t for ye Rag.ls ye 60th Reg.t — Adj.t for ye Provensials ye N. York Reg.t

Field Off.r for ye Provensials Col: Angel.

Gen^ll Lymans orders. That there be a Detachment of 220 men properly officerd from ye Provensial Troops to peraid tomorow morning at 6 oClock in order to March to Lake George & to Take 2 Days provision with them.

Fort Edward Octr 21st 1757.
Parole *Taunton*.
G. O. Field Off^r tomorow Maj^r Fletcher.
Adj^t for ye Ragulars ye Independants. Adj^t for the Provensials ye Rhod-Island Reg^t.
Col: Pason Field Off^r for ye Provensials.
For ye future when ye Guards march off from the Peraid, ye Rear Ranks are to Close to ye Front & they are to wheel to ye right by Divisions. ye Front Rank of Each Division is to Step of with ye Rear Rank of ye Division before them & ye Senter & Rear Ranks of Each Division are not to march of with ye Front Rank of their Respective Divisions but to

Step of with ye Front & Rear of ye Right before them.

After Orders. The 17th & Inniskilling Reg^t are to be Musterd tomorow at 12 oClock, & ye 35th & Royl Amarican Reg^t & Independant Companys are to take all ye Guards tomorow.

The 35th & Royl Amarican Reg^t & Independant Companys are to be Musterd on Sunday in ye forenoon. ye 17th & Inniskilling Reg^t are to take all ye Guards.

N. B. The Same party y^t was orderd for Saratoge to Day, to march tomorow with ye Teems Arrivd.

R. O. Ensⁿ Parsons for Guard Tomorow.

Fort Edward Octr 22nd 1757.

Parole *Darby*.

G. P. Field Off^r for tomorow Lt Col. Morris.

Adj^t for ye Rag^{ls} ye 17th Reg^{t.} Adj^t for ye Provensials ye Massachusetts Reg^{t.}

GENERAL ORDERS OF 1757

Col. Glayser Field off^r for ye Provensials.

Fort Edward Octr 23rd 1757
Parole *Dover*.

G. O. Field Off^r for tomorow Maj^r Prevost.

Adj^t for ye Ragulars ye Inniskilling Reg^{t.} Adj^t for ye Provensials ye Connecticutt Reg^{t.}

Col: Angel Field Off^r for ye Provensials.

The workmen Employed by ye Engineer are to be Furnish.d by ye Ragular Troops till further orders & ye Provensial Troops ar to furnish whatever men Shall be Demanded by Ensⁿ Parsons (of ye Connecticutt Reg^{t.}) till ye Bridge over to ye Island is finished. All ye hand Hatchets y^t have been Deliver.d out to ye Provensials by Mr. Euens Clerk of Ordnance Stores are to be Returnd to him as Soon as Possable.

A List of ye Names of ye Women belonging to Each Corp to be given into yͤ Genˡˡ Emediately Specifying yͤ Companys to which they belong.

A Copy of an Advertisement Sent up by Capt. Christy A. D. Q. M. Genˡˡ·

Whereas two Canadian Prisoners Lecoign & Leforge confind in yͤ Fort at Albany on Suspicion of carrying on a Corrispondancy with yͤ Enimy found means to Escape on yͤ 16ᵗʰ Currt in yͤ Night. This is to give notice to all his Majestys Subjects who Shall Apprehend & bring them to Albany Shall Receive 20£ N. York Currancy Emediately paid or 10£ N. York Currency for one of them. All offʳˢ Civel or Military are Desired & Required to be Aiding & Assisting in Apprehending & Securing sᵈ Lecoign & Leyforge by Comᵈ of the Genll.

Gabˡ Christy A. D. Q. M. Genˡˡ

R. O. Capt. Fitch & Ensn Tracy for Guard. Ensⁿ Baldwain for yͤ Saratoge Comᵈ·

Fort Edward Octr 24ᵗʰ 1757.
Parole *Lincoln.*

G. O. Field Off*r* for tomorow Maj*r* Darbe.

Adj*t* for y*e* Ragulars y*e* 35th Reg*t.* Adj*t* for y*e* Provensials y*e* N. York Reg*t.*

Col. Pason Field Off*r* for y*e* Provensial.

R. O. Ens*n* Minor for Guard.

Fort Edward Oct*r* 25, 1757.

Parole *Newark*.

Field Off*r* for tomorow Maj*r* Fletcher.

Adj*t* for y*e* Rag*ls* y*e* 60*th* Reg*t.* Adj*t* for y*e* Provensials the Rhode Island Reg*t.*

Field Off*r* for y*e* Provensial Col. Glayser.

R. O. Capt: Slapp & L*t* Wells for Guard tomorow.

Josiah Smith of Capt: Slaps Company is Restored to be a Searjant in s*d* Company & is to be Obayd as Such.

Fort Edward Oct*r* 26*th* 1757.

Parole *Stafford*.

Field Off^r for tomorow Lt Col: Morris.

Adj^t for ye Rag^ls ye Independant Companys. Adj^t for ye Provensials ye Massachusetts Reg^t.

Field Off^r for ye Provensials Col. Angel.

The working partys orderd for ye A. D. Q. M. G^ll are to carry their Days Provisions with them.

The provensial Troops will Fire on ye Island this afternoon.

R. O. Lieu^t John Durke for Guard tomorow.

Fort Edward Octr 27th 1757.

Parole *Cheshier*

Field Off^r for tomorow Maj^r Provost.

Adj^t for ye Rag^ls ye 17th Reg^t. — Adj^t for ye Provensials ye Connecticutt Reg^t.

Field Off^r for ye Provensials Mj^r Pason.

R. O. Capt Jeffery for Guard tomorow.

Fort Edward Oct[r] 28th 1757.

Parole *Marlow*.

Field Off[r] tomorow Maj[r] Darbe.

Adj[t] for y[e] Rag[ls] y[e] Inniskilling Reg[t.] Adj[t] for y[e] Provensials y[e] N. York Reg[t.]

Field Off[r] for y[e] Provensials Col. Glayser.

N. B. The party from y[e] Connecticutts is to continue 4 Days & Cr: will be given them in y[e] Gen[ll] Roster.

R. O. L[t] Simons for Guard tomorow.

Fort Edward Oct[r] 29th 1757.

Parole *Eye*.

Field Off[r] for tomorow Maj[r] Fletcher Adjt for y[e] Rag[ls] 35th Reg[t.] Adj[t] for y[e] Provensials y[e] Rhod Island Reg[t.]

Field Off[r] for y[e] Provensials Col. Angel.

Fort Edward Oct[r] 30th 1757.

Parole *Sandwich*.

Field Off[r] for tomorow L[t] Col. Morris.

Adj^t for y^e Ragulars y^e Royal Amarican Reg$^{t.}$ Adj^t for y^e Provensials y^e Massachusetts Reg$^{t.}$

Field Off^r for y^e Provensials Maj^r Pason.

R. O. Capt: Wells & Lt Elmer for Guard tomorow.

Fort Edward Octr 31st 1757.

Parole *Salfash*.

G. O. Field offr for tomorow Maj^r Prevost.

Adj$^{t.}$ for y^e Independant Companys. Adj^t for the Provensials y^e Connecticutt Reg$^{t.}$

Field Off^r for y^e provensials Col. Glayser.

R. O. Capt: Gallup & Lt Fitch for Guard tomorow.

Fort Edward Novr 1st 1757

Parole *Rygate*.

G. O. Field Off^r tomorow Maj^r Darbe

Adj^t for y^e Rag^{ls} y^e 17th.—Adj^t for y^e Provensials the N. York Reg$^{t.}$

Field Off^r for y^e Provensials Col: Glayser.

Fort Edward Novr 2nd 1757.

Parole *Beverly*.

G. O. Field Off^r for tomorrow Maj^r Fletcher.

Adjt for y^e Rag^ls y^e 35th Reg^t. Adjt for y^e Provensials y^e Rhod Island Reg^t.

Field Off^r for y^e Provensials Maj^r Pason.

Whenever his Excelency ye Earl of Loudoun shall Arrive the Lines are to Turn out at ye Head of their Respective Encampents & Draw up according to His Royal Highness the Dukes orders. The 17th Regt is to have a Sub^n 1 Searj^t 1 Corp. & 30 men ready to turn out at a Minutes warning as a Guard upon ye Earl of Loudoun.—

Each Corp is to have an Orderly Searj^t Ready for ye Earl of Loudoun & ye Adj^t Gen^ll when ever Sent for by ye Maj^r Brig-Aid.

G^ll L^ns O. That all ye Commissiond

& Non-Commissiond Off[rs] & Souldiers belonging to y[e] Several Provensial Corps on y[e] Island to hold them Selves in Readiness to turn out at a Minuts warning at y[e] head of their Respective Reg[ts] this afternoon. The Souldiers without their arms.

R. O. Searj[t] Epaphras Not of Capt. Whittlecy Company in Gen[ll] Lymans Reg[t] is Appointed Searj[t.] Maj[r] in s[d] Reg[t] & is to be obayd as Such.

Lieu[t] Billings for Guard tomorrow

Fort Edward Nov[r] 3rd 1757.

Parole *Arunder*

G. O. Field Off[r] for tomorow L[t] Col. Morris.

Adj[t] for y[e] 60th Reg[t.] — Adj[t] for y[e] Provensials y[e] Massachusetts Re[t.]

Field Off[r] for y[e] Provensials Col. Glayser.

A Return to be given in Emmediately to y[e] Maj[r] Brig Aid from Each Corp of y[e] Number of men they have to send from their Hospitals to Albana.—The Cirgions of Each Corp are all ways to Attend them Selves & se their own Sick properly in ye Waggons.

Upon ye Arrival of ye Earl of Loudoun ye Guns will be Fired.

R. O. Capt: Hitchcock for Guard tomorow & Lt Huntley for ye Saratoge Command.

Fort Edward Novr 4th 1757.

Parole *Brentford*

G. O. Field Officer for tomorow Maj^r Prevost.

Adj^t for ye Reg^{ls} ye Independant Comp^{ys}—Adj^t for ye Provensials ye Connecticutt Reg^t.

Field Off^r for ye Provensials Col: Angel.

R. O. Lt Nichols for Guard tomorow.

Fort Edward Novr 5th 1757.

Parole *Malden*.

G. O. Field Off^r for tomorow Maj^r Darbe.

Adjt for yͤ Ragls 17th Regt. —Adjᵗ for yᵉ Provensuals yᵉ N. York Regt.

Field Offr for yᵉ Provensials Majr Pason.

The out Centerys from yᵉ Guard in Camp are not to allow any Souldier to pass them without a Pass from yᵉ Offr of yᵉ Guard. & yᵉ Patroles from yᵉ Gd upon yᵉ Right & left of yᵉ Lines are to make prisoners all Souldiers yᵗ they find beyond yᵉ Advans'd Centerys who are to be Confin.d & tried for Disobaying orders.

Gll Lns O. that any person who Shall be found Guilty of fireing off Crackers or Squibs in yᵉ Provensial Camp Shall be Emediately Confin.d for Disobaying orders & Embazling yᵉ Kings Stores.

The Searjt & Corplls of Each Corp are to Se yᵗ their men who are orderd for any Comd are acqt 24 Rounds of powdr. & Ball before they march them into yᵉ Grand Peraid.

R. O. Capt. Durke & Lt Parsons for Guard tomorow.

GENERAL ORDERS OF 1757

Fort Edward Novr 6th 1757.

Parole *Harwick*.

G. O. Field Off^r tomorow Lt Col. Morris.

Adj^t for y^e Rag^{ls} ye Inniskilling Reg$^{t.}$—Adj^t for the Provensials y^e Rhodisland Reg$^{t.}$

Field Off^r for y^e Provensials Col. Glayser.

The 3rd Battallion of y^e Royal Amarican Reg^t is to March tomorow. Y^e Off^{rs} & men of y^t Corp now on Duty are to come of Emediately after Gunfiring tomorrow morning No huts to be burnt upon any account.

The piq^t till further orders is to be furnish.d from ye 17th & 27th Reg^{ts} & to consist of one Capt: 3 Sub^s 4 Searj^{ts} 9 Corp^{lls} & 148 men.—Ye Piq^t is to peraid tomorow morning at gunfiring & ye Capt. with two Subs: 3 Searj^{ts}: 5 Corp^{lls} & 91 men is to march to ye Left of ye Lines to Relieve ye Capt: of ye Guard there the other Sub^n with one Searj^t 4 Corp^{ls} & 57 men is to march & Relieve ye Off^r on yᵉ Right of yᵉ Lines & for yᵉ future yᵉ Posts of yᵉ Camp are to be Augmented by yᵉ Piqᵗ & Divided as above. Yᵉ 17ᵗʰ & 27ᵗʰ Regᵗ are to Augment their Quarter Guards with one Sub. 1 Searjᵗ 1 Corpˡ & 30 men Each. & to mount every morning at Troop beeting.

 R. O. Capt. Fitch for Guard tomorow.

Fort Edward Novʳ 7ᵗʰ 1757.
 Parole *Loudoun.*
 G. O. Field Offʳ for tomorow Majʳ Darbe
 Adjᵗ for yᵉ Ragˡˢ yᵉ 17th Regᵗ· Adjᵗ for yᵉ Provensials yᵉ Massachusetts Regᵗ·
 Field Offʳ for yᵉ Provensials Col. Angel
 R. O. Ensⁿ Chick for Guard tomorow
 Corpˡ Kent of Genˡˡ Lymans Company is Appointed Searjᵗ & Osaah Willcockson is Appointed Corpˡˡ and both to be obay.d as Such.
 A Return to be given in to yᵉ Adjᵗ Emediately of yᵉ Names of all yᵉ Artifis-

ers of Each Company in ye Connecticutt Reg^t.

Fort Edward Novr 8th 1757.

Parole *London*.

G. O. Field Off^r tomorow Lt Col. Haviland.

Adj^t for ye Rag^ls ye 27th Reg^t. — Adj^t for the Provensials ye Connecticutt Reg^t.

Field Off^r for ye Provensials Maj^r Pason.

All ye Folentears belonging to ye Ragular Troops & now with ye Rangers are to join their Respective Corps as Soon as they can.

The 17th Reg^t & ye Detachment from the Inniskilling Reg^t y^t are to be Posted at Saratoge & Still Water are to March tomorow.

G^l L^ns O. That ye men belonging to ye Provensial Troops take perticular Cair not to pull Down or Distroy any of their Hutts upon Penalty of Staying here all Winter.

The men y^t Ensⁿ Sumner has a List of belonging to ye Connecticutt Reg^t are to march to Saratoge tomorow morning by 10 oClock.

Fort Edward Novr 9th 1757.

Parole *Barwick*.

R. O. At a Gen^{ll} Assembly of ye Governer & Company of ye Colony of Connecticutt holden at Hartford ye 2nd Thursday of May A. D. 1757.

Whereas ye Reg^t Raisd in this Colony ye present Year to act in Conjunction with his Majestys Ragular Troops under ye Com^d of his Excelency ye Earl of Loudoun in ye Next Campaign are furnish.d with ye Kings arms for which Recaits are taken of ye Respective Comp^{ys} who are accordingly chargable with ye Same to be Returned According to Such orders as Shall be given by ye Commander in Chief of his Majestys forces in North America to Such Person or Persons as Shall be appointed by this Assembly to Receive ye Same. Therefor it is Resolv.d by this

Assembly y^t Andrew Burr of Fairfield Esqr· Col: Gurd^n Saltonstall of New London, Col. Jabez Hamlin of Middle Town Maj^r David Whitney of Canaan & Mist^{rs} Chancy Whittlecy & Joseph Church of Hartford are appointed and Impowered to Receive ye S^d Arms from ye S^d Capt^s· & give proper Receits for ye Same & keep Distinct Accounts of Each Capt^s Company & keep ye Same in good order until further Directions be given them by ye Assembly.

George Wyllys Sec^y

A true Coppy.

The Commanding Off^{rs} of ye Several Companys in ye Connecticutt Regt are to take perticular Cair not to have any Bills Contracted upon ye Governments Credit upon their march home.

The following Detachment to be Drafted in to Capt. Putnam's Ranging Company this Afternoon. (viz) Gen^{ll} Lymans Company 3 men Capt. Gallup 5, Cap: Wellss 2. Capt. Whittlecys 2.

GENERAL ORDERS OF 1757

Fort Edward Nov. 10th 1757.

Parole *Loudoun*.

Col. Haviland's orders. All ye Massachusetts Rhod-Islanders & Connecticutts (Except ye two companys of ye Connecticut Rangers) to hold them Selves in Readiness to march as soon as Carriage can be provided. the men of these Corps now on Duty are to be Relieved by ye N. Yorkers.

Majr Rogers is to order a Guard of Rangers to post proper sentery from it, on ye Live Stock Garden & Fire wood & no Sort of thing to be taken out of ye Garden without proper leave from Col: Haviland & no fire wood to be touch.d as they will be answerable for it & ye offender punished with the utmost Severity.

The guard at ye Island End of ye Bridge not to Suffer any man to pass over toard ye Garden after the Retreat.—And any Preson yt is known (Either of ye Troops in Garson or on ye Island) to pul down any part of a Hut on Either Side ye water will be brought to a Court Mareschal for ye Same unless he Shall have perticular leave for it.

Fort Edward Novr 10th 1757.
    Parole *Hampton.*
The Massachusetts & Rhodislanders to march Emediately. they are to apply to Mr. Lesley for carriage & proceed according to ye orders they have Recd from Lord Loudoun.

Fort Edward Novr 12th 1757.
    Parole *Inverness.*

Fort Edward Novr 13th 1757.
    Parole *Sterling.*

Fort Edward Novr 14th 1757.
    Parole *Prestonpan.*

Fort Edward Novr 15th 1757.
    Parole *Colloden.*

Fort Edward Novr 16th 1757.
    Parole *Perth.*

Fort Edward Novr 17th 1767.
   Parole *Tweede*.

Fort Edward Novr 18th 1757.
   Parole *Callen*.

INDEX

INDEX

Adams, Doctor, 79
Adjutants and orders, 31
Alarms, 21, 22, 24, 50
Albany, detachment for, 66
Ammunition, 42
Anderson, John, 80
Andrus, Jacob, Captain, 95
Angel, S., Colonel, 110
Arms, return of, 41, 133
Articles of War, 9, 20, 81
Artificers, return of, 131
Assembly of Connecticut, 133
Attack, report on, 53
Axe parties, 102, 107
Bark, gathering, 20
Bartman, George, Captain, 33, 41
Beer, brewing of, 70
Bellew, Captain, 116
Billings, Lieutenant, 104
Breach of Order, 3, 9
Bridge to Island, 120
Burr, Andrew, 134
Burying-ground, 47

Camp, cleaning of, 25, 29, 33, 83, 105
Carpenters, 88
Carpenters, ship, 40, 58, 59
Cartridges, 5, 8, 28, 37, 40, 45
Carver, J., Captain, 110
Castle, Lieutenant, 26, 82
Centries, punishment, 67
Certificates for hospital, 54
Charters, Captain, 93
Chimneys, 106
Christie, Gabriel, Captain, 35, 36, 121
Church, Joseph, 134
Cobb, James, 95
Commissaries, 69
Comstock, Josiah, Sergeant, 49
Connecticut, 47, 102, 133
Connolly, Roger, 80
Coser, Joseph, 94
Crackers, firing of, 129
Cunningham, Captain, 27
Dalyell, Lieutenant, 55

INDEX

Delancey, Captain, 79
Deserters, 68, 70
Dickinson, Sergeant, 89
Dike, Gideon, 95
Dorman, Henry, 79, 82
Dress of men, 47, 49, 63
Drummers, 91
Dun, John, 80
Durkee, John, Lieutenant, 4, 16, 17, 30, 47
Durkee, Robert, Lieutenant, 16
Ewings, Clerk of Ordnance, 107, 120
Exercise of men, 49, 78, 103
Fascines, 34
Firelocks, repair of, 41
Firing of pieces, 58, 72, 97
Fitch, Captain, 10, 26, 30
Fleming, Francis, 79
Fletcher, Major, 21, 25, 27, 28, 75, 82
Flints, 13
Fort Ann, 17, 20
Fort Edward, 10, 49
Fort William Henry, 54
Furniss, Contractor, 39
Gallup, Ben Adam, Captain, 12, 17
Gaming, 92
Garden, 14, 135
Glayser, B., Colonel, 92
Goff, Colonel, 26
Gordon, Engineer, 71
Guards, 118

Guards at Fort Edward, 15
Guards at Scortercook, 4, 6, 7
Half Moon, 56, 57
Hamlin, Jabez, 134
Handee, David, Corporal, 90
Harding, Lieutenant, 47
Harrison, Lieutenant-Colonel, 96, 107
Haviland, Lieutenant-Colonel, 93
Haviland, Captain, 135
Hierlihy, Timothy, 102
Hitchcock, Captain, 47, 74
Hogaboom's, 1, 3
Hospital, 54, 127
Houses, necessary, 34, 46, 91
Howard, Benjamin, Ensign, 16
Howe, Lord, 66, 67
Hull, Silley, 80
Humphreys, Lieutenant, 17, 30
Hunting, 75
Huts, 113, 132, 135
Independent Companies, 46
Indians, 12, 14, 17, 44, 60, 74
Inspection, 23, 55, 64
Invalids, 79
Island, occupation of, 86
Island, rules for, 88
Jeffery, John, Captain, 16, 30, 82, 85
Johnson, Sir William, 14, 17
Johnson, 60
Jones, John, 80
Kent, Corporal, 131

INDEX

Kim, John, 115
Knowles, *see* Notes
Lake George, detachment to, 118
Larned, Captain, 84
Lecoign, 121
Leforge, 121
Lesley, 11, 35, 46
Letters, 33, 43, 90
Levi, Garshom, 114
Leynord, George, 115
Liquor, sale of, 44, 54
Littler, Captain, 55
Loudoun, Earl of, 126
Lyman, Phineas, 1, 86
McDuffy, John, 116
Marsey, Major, 86
Maunsel, Captain, 75
Minor, Ensign, 4, 9, 17
Morris, Roger, 40
Mullen, William, 80
Murphy (Murfa), Gardiner, 71
Muster rolls, 8, 19, 26, 31, 71, 112
New Hampshire troops, 25
Nichols, Nicholas, 13, 47
Noles, Lieutenant, 99
Nott, Epaphras, Sergeant, 85, 127
Odea, Doctor, 79
Officer of the day, duties of, 66
Officers, rank of, 77
Officers to wear swords, 44
Ord, Captain, 41
Panics, 111

Parade, 2, 101
Parole, 87, 94
Parsons, Ensign, 120
Patrol, night, 70
Payson, N., Major, 75
Picquets, 22, 37
Pike, David, Sergeant, 87, 106
Pioneers, 113
Porter, Elijah, Ensign, 4, 13
Powder-horns, 65
Prayers, 79
Prevost, Major, 63, 85
Prisoners, 43, 69, 76, 87, 121
Provisions, 24
Putnam, Captain, 8
Randal, Benjamin, 80
Rangers, 16, 19, 39, 50, 58, 67, 70, 84, 85, 105
Rank of officers, 77
Returns, 27, 40, 46, 59, 62, 64, 76, 102
Rhodes, John, 114
Rice, Llewellen, 79, 82
Rider, John, 81
Ripley, Charles, 106
Ripley, Quartermaster, 91
Rogers, Major, 135
Royal Americans, 130
Rum, 14
Russell, Lieutenant, 108, 110
Sailors, return of, 40, 58, 59
Saltonstall, Gurdon, 134
Saratoga, 11, 48
Sawyers, 73
Scouts, 60

143

INDEX

Sentinels, 21, 67
Simons, Lieutenant, 4, 17
Slapp, John, Captain, 12, 13, 28, 30
Smith, Josiah, Sergeant, 112, 122
Stillwater, 48, 85
Stoughton, John, Lieutenant, 9, 13, 16
Strolling, 27, 56, 129
Suttlers, regulations, 35, 54
Teams, 60
Tents, 32, 62
Thear, Peter, 81
Thody, Captain, 90
Timber, 18, 71, 74
Titcomb, Lieutenant, 61
Tools, 28
Tuttle, Jonathan, 32
Vannigan, Lieutenant, 40
Wall, Captain, 108, 110
Waterman, Jedediah, Lieutenant, 9, 12
Webb, Daniel, Major-General, 29, 87, 90
Welch, 15
Wells, Captain, 30
Wells, Samuel, Lieutenant, 13, 28, 47
Welsh, Patrick, 78
West, Captain, 84
Westerman, Andrew, 115
Whitney, David, 134
Whittlesey, Aaron, Captain, 3, 9, 82
Whittlesey, Chauncy, 134
Willcockson, Osaah, Corporal, 131
Women, enlisted, 41, 120
Woodall, Captain, 42
Young, Frederic, 114
Young, Lieutenant-Colonel, 42

www.ingramcontent.com/pod-product-compliance
Lightning Source LLC
Chambersburg PA
CBHW030339170426
43202CB00010B/1175